# KIDS FIGHT EXTINCTION

## How to Be a #2minutesuperhero

This is for you: the **#2minutesuperhero**

First US edition 2024

Library of Congress Catalog Card Number 2023944645
ISBN 978-1-5362-3400-8

23 24 25 26 27 28 LEO 10 9 8 7 6 5 4 3 2 1

Printed in Heshan, Guangdong, China

This book was typeset in Myriad Pro.
The illustrations were created digitally.

Candlewick Press
99 Dover Street
Somerville, Massachusetts 02144

www.candlewick.com

# KIDS FIGHT EXTINCTION

## Act Now to Be a #2minuteSuperhero

### MARTIN DOREY

#### ILLUSTRATED BY TIM WESSON

CANDLEWICK PRESS

# CONTENTS

# ARE YOU READY TO BE A SUPERHERO?

# SUPERHEROES SAVE THE ANIMALS!

Are you ready to save animals
and be a #2minutesuperhero?
Of course you are!
Right. What can you do in two minutes?
Tidy your room? Maybe. Drink a glass of
juice? Probably. Brush your teeth? Just.
Help save animals from extinction?
Definitely.
Two minutes is all you need to do
something amazing, such as . . .
Give nature a hand.
Change your habits.
Save the planet.

# NATURE NEEDS YOU

Our planet is facing a crisis. Lots of plants, mammals, birds, and insects are facing extinction. That means they will die out if we don't help them. Once they are gone they will be gone forever.

It's going to take a huge group effort to fight extinction and help save nature—starting with each of us.

That's YOU.

Why you? Because, believe it or not, you have the power to make a difference. You don't need a cape or a mask or to be able to fly or fight villains in an intergalactic spaceship to help solve the crisis. You just have to be you.

Because you've got what it takes.

This book will show you how, in just a few minutes, you can help to fight extinction, restore nature, take care of animals and plants, and save the planet. And—while doing it—become a **#2minutesuperhero**.

Not a bad trade-off, right?

Ready to save me and be a superhero?

# WHY YOU ARE THE IDEAL #2MINUTESUPERHERO

You have the power to help fight extinction, from your brilliant brain to your superhero smile. The most important thing to remember is: everything you do makes a difference in helping to save the planet, no matter how small.

You have the power to make changes in your world! Go, you!

Your ideas are your greatest tools! Thinking about how to solve problems is a true superpower.

You can stick up for all the plants and animals that don't have a voice.

Spread the word and advocate for plants and animals.

## SOMETHING TO REMEMBER

There will be times when it'll be easy to see the results of your actions. There may be other times when you won't see the effects of your hard work. In these times it's important to remember that everything you do matters and will have some kind of impact, in some way, at some point, somewhere in the world.

# ME AND MY #2MINUTEMISSION

Before we get started, I would like to tell you a bit about myself.
My name is Martin. I am an eco-activist, beach cleaner, and writer.
Many years ago I started picking up litter on my local beach.
I posted pictures of that litter on social media using a new hashtag
**#2minutebeachclean**. Lots of people joined in, and before I knew
it the whole thing went global!

My beach cleanup idea turned into a nonprofit company that
aims to save the planet two minutes at a time. The experience made
me believe that anyone can make a difference and that everyone
has the power to change the world through small actions. Why?
Because lots of small actions add up to make a BIG difference.

You can be a **#2minutesuperhero**. If you make little changes in
your life, you could be making life better for a mammal, insect, or
bird somewhere. You might never see the effect. But it does matter!

**EVERYDAY SUPERHERO**

**Name:** Martin

**Job:** Writer and activist

**Superpower:** Using words to get
people to do good stuff

**How you fight extinction:** I pick up
litter, write books, plant trees, and
ride my bike.

**Top tip:** Everybody can make a
difference.

**Hates:** Wasting energy

**Loves:** Solar showers

MARTIN

## YOUR EXTINCTION TOOLBOX

Fighting extinction isn't going to be easy. But you have a huge supply of tools and actions you can use to help. When a superhero uses them wisely—and we'll find out how later—they make you invincible (or very difficult to argue with, which is just as good IMHO).

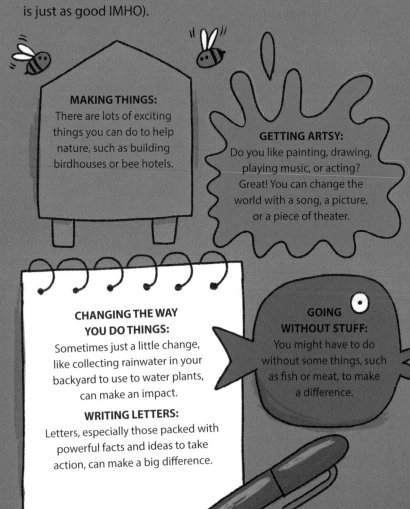

**MAKING THINGS:**
There are lots of exciting things you can do to help nature, such as building birdhouses or bee hotels.

**GETTING ARTSY:**
Do you like painting, drawing, playing music, or acting? Great! You can change the world with a song, a picture, or a piece of theater.

**CHANGING THE WAY YOU DO THINGS:**
Sometimes just a little change, like collecting rainwater in your backyard to use to water plants, can make an impact.

**GOING WITHOUT STUFF:**
You might have to do without some things, such as fish or meat, to make a difference.

**WRITING LETTERS:**
Letters, especially those packed with powerful facts and ideas to take action, can make a big difference.

**THE MEDIA:**
Newspapers, websites, and TV channels can be really powerful. The media can help you share your story with other superheroes in the making.

**GOING ONLINE:**
Ideas can travel around the world superfast online. If it's safe, and if your parents or caregivers let you, going online can be another powerful tool.

**BUYING THINGS (OR NOT BUYING THEM):**
Companies that are harming nature don't deserve your money. Spend it on the good guys instead!

**TALKING:**
Chatting with your friends is a great way to change things. The more people helping, the faster the change.

**MAKING POSTERS:**
Share your message far and wide. Put posters in your window at home and at school and in local businesses, if they agree.

**PROTESTING:**
As long as you do it legally and peacefully, protesting can be a great way of getting your voice heard. Attending a rally, where people come together in a group, or even sitting outside your school, like Greta Thunberg did outside Swedish parliament, is a form of protest. You could organize your own or join one (with your parents or caregivers).

# HOW TO USE THIS BOOK

♠ This book contains a series of **MISSIONS**. Each will help you to understand extinction, the natural world, and how we fit into it. Crucially, each mission explains what you can do to fight extinction and the areas of your life where you **CAN** make a difference.

♠ The big missions all contain **2-MINUTE MISSIONS**.

♠ These are tasks that are fun and help the environment. Each task is worth superhero points and will require you to use something in your toolbox.

♠ Some of the **2-MINUTE MISSIONS** are hard. Some are easy. The harder missions will earn you more points. Some will also take longer than two minutes!

♠ After each completed mission, write down the number of points you've earned.

♠ Once you have finished the book, add up your points to get your final score. Turn to page 124 to find out what kind of superhero you are.

## ARE YOU READY?

Sign here. Before you start, I need to know that you are committed to saving nature. Will you take the pledge?

I solemnly pledge my allegiance to nature.

I will fight extinction through my actions and will take **2** minutes of every day to help nature, the natural world, and the animals that share our planet.

Training approved by:

Founder of the #2minutebeachclean

# ABOUT THE AUTHOR

Hello. I am Martin Dorey. I'm a surfer, writer, beach lover, and anti-plastic and climate change activist. I live near the sea in Cornwall, England, with my partner, Lizzy, who is also known as Dr. Seaweed. She's a gardener and botanist who helps me understand plants and photosynthesis and all that exciting stuff! My children, Maggie and Charlotte, live down the road from me with their dog, Bob. Maggie is a lifeguard and Charlotte makes a lot of her own clothes. I like surfing, walking, being outside, and trying to grow vegetables. I also cook a lot, especially when I'm in my camper van. I also like riding my bike, cleaning beaches, and waking up to sunny days by the sea with the people I love the most.

# ABOUT THE 2 MINUTE FOUNDATION

**The 2 Minute Foundation (www.2minute.org)** is a charity that is devoted to cleaning up the planet two minutes at a time. The idea is very simple: each time you go to the beach, the park, or anywhere at all, take two minutes to pick up litter, take a picture of it, and then post it to social media to inspire others to do the same.

In 2014, we set up a network of eight Beach Clean Stations around Cornwall, England, that make it easy for people to pick up litter at the beach. We now have more than one thousand of them! Some are even made from the plastic we picked up off the beach! We have thousands of followers who help the planet every day by cleaning beaches, cutting out plastic from their lives, or picking up litter from the streets where they live.

*With thanks to:*
Lizzy, my semi-tame botanist (and best mate);
Tim Wesson;
Daisy, Charlie, Laurissa, Faith, and everyone at Walker Books;
Tim Bates at Peters Fraser and Dunlop Literary Agents;
the **2 Minute Foundation** family;
Chris Hines;
and anyone else who has made an effort, no matter how small,
to make a difference.

# YOUR MISSIONS START NOW...

# GET TO KNOW EXTINCTION

Welcome to the training school for superheroes!

It's like a school but not like a school. For a start, it's got animals, plants, and even a dinosaur. And there are no desks or lessons, just a lot of fun stuff to do and missions to complete.

At Superhero School you will learn all about extinction, why it's important to fight it, and why fighting for one animal means you fight for all animals.

It's not easy to understand extinction in just a few lines. In fact, it's a bit complicated at times. But bear with me, because this will help you to understand why we need to act and how we can use our superhero powers (and by that I mean our ideas, hearts, and voices) to start to fight extinction.

It's a complex story and has sad parts and happy parts, and did I mention the dinosaurs?

Let's start at the beginning.

## WHAT IS EXTINCTION?

Extinction is the complete disappearance of a type of fish, bird, plant, mammal, insect, or reptile from Earth. It is what happens when the last of its kind (or species) dies.

Extinction is a natural process and has been happening since life on Earth began.

Think of the dinosaurs. They lived on Earth for about 165 million years and then became extinct after what scientists believe was a major event—an asteroid strike, perhaps— around sixty-five million years ago. Most of them were wiped out, with the exception of those that went on to become birds. (It is amazing to think, isn't it, that the birds in your backyard are descended from dinosaurs!)

# INTERVIEW WITH A DINOSAUR

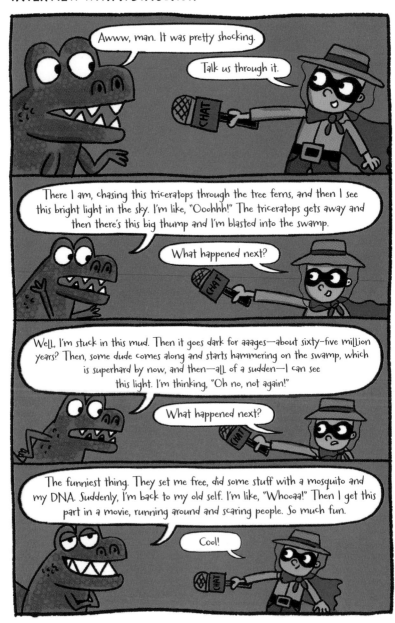

## FASCINATING FOSSILS

What we know about dinosaurs comes from fossils, which are their preserved skeletons. Fossils are formed when an animal or plant dies and is covered in mud or ash, which then turns, over millions of years, into rock and stone.

There are lots of places to find fossils! You can dig them out of the ground, but you may also find them in surprising places too. You can see fossils everywhere, even in the stone used to make buildings in your town or city.

YOUR 2-MINUTE MISSION: Use your superhero ability of discovery to go on a fossil hunt! 10 POINTS
1. Visit your local museum.
2. Look for stones in your town. For examples, check out: www.londonpavementgeology.co.uk
3. If you can, get your family or caregivers to take you on a fossil hunt in an area that has lots of stones.

## IF EXTINCTION IS NATURAL, WHAT'S THE PROBLEM?

Before today there were five events that caused mass extinctions. This is when lots of the creatures on Earth died out. Some of these events caused more than 90 percent of all animals to die. One of these mass extinctions wiped out (almost) all the dinosaurs. Others wiped out plants and sea creatures. Some of these events were caused by massive catastrophes like asteroids or volcanic eruptions, but some happened over millions of years.

In "normal" times we would expect species to go extinct for all kinds of reasons, but what is happening now is that many more species are threatened with extinction than is typical. In fact, the rate of extinction, according to the World Wildlife Fund, is about one thousand times higher than it should be.

That's scary, huh?

**YES. THEY ARE RELATED!**

Great-great-great-great-great-great-great-grandma!

**YOUR 2-MINUTE MISSION:** Go to the park, the woods, or even just your backyard. Sit quietly for a couple of minutes and see if you can spot a dinosaur. (CLUE: Birds are distant relatives of dinosaurs.) 5 POINTS

## WHY IS EXTINCTION BAD?

When you think about extinction, you may only think about losing exciting—and scary—creatures like *Tyrannosaurus rex*, but extinction is a modern problem that is bad for all of us.

When an animal, like a tiger or rhinoceros, goes extinct, it means that it is lost forever. Obviously it's bad for that species, but it's also bad for the species that it shares a habitat with, that depend on it, or that are otherwise influenced by it.

If we allow this to happen, then all the ecosystems (these are like mini planets within a planet) that depend on those species will collapse, threatening the safety of our food, water, and societies.

Lots of things cause extinctions. You can read about them later.

**SCARY FACT:** Between 1970 and 2014 the planet lost, on average, 60 percent of its populations of mammals, birds, fish, reptiles, and amphibians.

25

## WHY STOP THE EXTINCTIONS?

Planet Earth is beautiful. It is our home. It is also home to millions of insects, birds, mammals, fish, reptiles, and plants. Each of us depends on others for food, shelter, water, and life. Earth's ecosystem has a delicate balance that is at risk if thousands of species are lost. Imagine a line of dominoes. When one falls, the rest go too.

Everything on Earth is related.

**HUMMINGBIRDS LOVE NECTAR BECAUSE:**
It's their food! Hummingbirds have evolved to be able to hover in front of flowers and use their long beaks to get access to the nectar, which is right inside the flower.

**FLOWERS LOVE HUMMINGBIRDS BECAUSE:**
When hummingbirds collect nectar from flowers, they also get pollen on their feathers, which they then spread on other plants. This helps with fertilization and plays a vital part in producing new plants.

**WITHOUT THE HUMMINGBIRDS:**
The plants wouldn't be able to reproduce and would die.

**WITHOUT THE PLANTS:**
The hummingbirds would die because they would have no food.

**IF YOU PROTECT THE FLOWERS:**
You also protect the hummingbirds.

## EXTINCT VERSUS FUNCTIONALLY EXTINCT

What's the difference? Functionally extinct is the way scientists describe types of animals that have so few members that they cannot recover.

Najin and Fatu are the last northern white rhinos. They are mother and daughter. There are no males left, which means that when Najin and Fatu die, the northern white rhino species will be extinct. It is very sad.

It makes me angry, because the last northern white rhinos were killed by poachers and loss of habitat. But it also makes me determined because there are other animals that we can save. And that's why we need to step up and make a difference, no matter how small.

## WHAT IS THE IUCN RED LIST?

This is a list of the most critically endangered animals, insects, birds, and fish on Earth. Currently, there are about 150,300 species on the Red List. It is compiled by the International Union for Conservation of Nature, an organization made up of around one thousand dedicated scientists and staff in more than fifty countries. They provide facts and information on endangered animals to compel governments to act.

## WHY DO WE NEED TO ACT NOW?

Today we are at a point in time when it's not too late to change. It's a really important moment for our planet. The United Nations has announced that around one million species are at risk of extinction now. They haven't gone extinct yet. It's too late for the northern white rhino (I'm still a bit sad about that) but not for millions of other species. That means we still have a chance.

If we act decisively to save nature, then we will all benefit. I'm sorry that it falls to your generation to do this important work when a lot of my generation stood around and let it happen.

But it's not all bad news. While we have a chance to change, we still have hope. And that's a reason to smile.

Now is the time to act. Shall we do it?

Yes!

# THE CAUSES OF EXTINCTION

In any fight, whether it's for more space on the sofa or the last scoop of ice cream, it's important that you, as a superhero, understand what the battle is for, why it's significant, and perhaps most importantly, what you can do about it.

What do we know? We know we are fighting for nature against extinction. But we also have to understand the causes of extinction in order to work out what we can do about it. Unless you can get to the root cause of the problem, you are only really treating the effects of the problem.

In the case of extinction, sadly, one of the main causes is how we, humans, treat our planet.

### GREAT NEWS!
Everything you do that's kind to the planet will help in the fight against extinction.

We've already talked a little bit about historical extinctions, which were caused by events like asteroid strikes. This is the kind of event that killed off the dinosaurs but that doesn't threaten us today. Plus, we can't do anything about it, other than learn from the experience. But dinosaurs are cool, right?

You might have heard scientists and newspapers talk about what is happening today as the "sixth mass extinction." There are lots of reasons why animals become extinct or are at risk of extinction. Some of these are caused by people, while others are the result of the way things change over time. What's worrying, as I have said before, is the rate at which the extinctions and changes are happening today. Because of us humans.

**❌ THE DEARLY DEPARTED ❌**

**Name:** Steggy

**Job:** Stegosaurus

**Superpower:** Having a spiky tail to ward off predators

**How extinction affects you:** Sadly I went extinct, possibly because I was unable to compete with other dinosaurs.

**Top tip:** Develop your skills instead of spikes if you want to survive.

**Hates:** That he wasn't a bird

**Loves:** Eating small bushes

**❌ STEGGY ❌**

## EXTINCTION BY NATURAL SELECTION

Lots of animals and plants have gone extinct during our planet's long history (four and a half billon years, in case you were wondering) for lots of reasons. One of these is natural selection, an idea coined by Charles Darwin to describe the natural way animals and plants evolve (and leave others behind).

## WHY DOES IT CAUSE EXTINCTION?

Natural selection is what we call it when species adapt and change to fit their environments. It also means that sometimes an animal dies out because it cannot compete anymore or can't adapt to changing climate, weather, or environment.

## YOUR IMPERFECT COUSIN

Did you know that there were lots of types of humans before us? Some of them were known as Neanderthals, and they lived as recently as forty thousand years ago. We aren't exactly sure why they went extinct, but it may be because they were outcompeted by modern humans (us). They had language, used tools, made fire, and hunted but may have been pushed into extinction because modern humans had better tools, hunting techniques, and ability to survive. They are often portrayed as unintelligent, but they weren't.

## TODAY'S EXTINCTION THREATS

We can't do anything about past extinctions. But we may be able to do something about those that are about to happen.

Your next task, then, is to get to know WHY they are happening.

## CHANGING CLIMATE AND WARMING SEAS

Climate change is having a huge effect on the natural world. It affects everything, from the creatures at the bottom of the ocean to insects and birds.

It's complicated, but it's about changing weather patterns caused by the greenhouse effect of gases such as carbon dioxide and methane emitted by human activity. The gases are causing the planet to warm up gradually, and this is causing the seas to warm up and weather patterns to change all across the planet.

## WHY IS IT CAUSING EXTINCTION?

Gases (mainly from burning fossil fuels) that are building in the atmosphere are causing the temperature of the planet to warm up. Even if you can't see greenhouse gases, they are a big problem that impacts all of us. Animals are struggling to survive. They can't find food and their homes are being destroyed by fires or flooding.

## HABITAT DESTRUCTION

If someone destroyed your home, how would you feel? Awful, right? That's exactly what is happening to lots of animals and plants all over the world. In fact, it's one of the most common reasons why animals are facing extinction. Humans are just too greedy and are taking up all the land for themselves!

The homes of animals and plants are being destroyed all over the world. Habitats are lost due to climate change, because of wildfires or flooding, or because jungle and woodland are being cleared to make way for farmland or towns and cities.

## WHY IS IT CAUSING EXTINCTION?

Some animals are so highly specialized that they can live in only one place. These are called endemic species, and if their homes get destroyed they have nowhere to go, nothing to eat, and no shelter.

## HUMAN ENCROACHMENT

What would happen if your town wanted to tear down your home and put in a parking lot? You wouldn't have anywhere to go! It's the same for animals whose lives have been disrupted by us. When humans take over the homes of animals or plants, it leaves them with nowhere else to go.

## WHY IS IT CAUSING EXTINCTION?

As our cities expand and the land we use to grow food and live on spreads out, we come into ever closer contact with animals and plants that were previously just our neighbors. Who do you think is affected most when humans encroach on the natural world? Sadly, it is usually the animals.

# DEFORESTATION

The forests are vital for the health of our planet because they provide a place for countless animals to live and also prevent flooding and erosion.

Through photosynthesis, trees provide a lot of the oxygen we need to breathe. They also store carbon, which is important in the fight against climate change, and they help reduce pollution in cities.

# WHY IS IT CAUSING EXTINCTION?

Deforestation is devastating for the animals living in the forest. When forests and trees get cut down for timber or are destroyed to make room for farms and crops, it has a terrible effect on our ecosystems, threatening the lives of animals and living things all over the world.

## HUMAN PREDATION AND POACHING

We've been eating and hunting animals for as long as we've been on the planet. Long ago we hunted for food or to defend ourselves from animals that were a threat to us, like lions, poisonous snakes, and bears. We also hunted animals for their products, like fur from seals or ivory from elephants.

Poaching is when animals are killed illegally for their fur, tusks, or skins. It is estimated that around thirty-five thousand African elephants are killed by poachers every year. Both African and Asian elephants, along with African lions, Grevy's zebras, and all rhino species are likely to go extinct in your lifetime unless we act.

## WHY IS IT CAUSING EXTINCTION?

Sadly, throughout human history we have killed animals either for food, fur, or sport. It's awful that so many animals have become endangered or extinct because of human cruelty and greed.

- Since the 1990s, 43 percent of the African lion population has disappeared.

- There are only about one thousand mountain gorillas left in Africa.

- Gray wolves in the US have been protected under the Endangered Species Act, which is helping them from becoming extinct; however, they are still endangered.

- The Steller's sea cow was hunted to extinction in 1768, just thirty years after it was discovered by humans.

- The passenger pigeon used to be the most abundant bird in North America, before it was hunted to extinction in the nineteenth century.

## KILLING FOR "SPORT"

Hunting for sport is when people kill animals just because they can. Some people like to kill animals for their skins or to hang trophies of the animals' heads on their wall.

Animals that are hunted for trophies are usually males that have big antlers, manes, or horns. Killing them has a disastrous effect on populations because it wipes out the strongest males from the breeding stock, making the species more vulnerable.

It is estimated that the African lion population has fallen by 43 percent in the last two decades and may now number fewer than twenty thousand. And yet African lions may legally be hunted in many countries.

**ALARMING FACT:** From 2004 to 2014 alone, hunters took home more than 1.7 million "trophies" from animals killed for "sport." More than two hundred thousand animals in danger of going extinct are hunted and killed every year.

## POLLUTION

Pollution can take many forms, whether it's from plastic, acid rain, industry, or agriculture. However, it is always something—a chemical or physical substance—that is toxic to the environment and upsets the natural balance of ecosystems, threatening thousands of species around the world.

## WHY IS IT CAUSING EXTINCTION?

Pollution, when it gets into contact with sensitive ecosystems, can cause damage to food, the air, water, or soil so that nothing can grow. In the case of plastic pollution, it can also kill animals if they eat it or get tangled in it.

**BAD NEWS!**
The flesh-footed shearwaters of Australia are one of many species endangered because of plastic. The adults feed at sea—picking up plastic instead of food—and give it to their chicks at their nests. The chicks then die because they have full stomachs but no nutrition. Some shearwater bird colonies have declined by as much as 50 percent while other colonies have disappeared altogether.

# PESTICIDES

Pesticides are chemicals or compounds that are used to kill insects or organisms that are harmful to cultivated plants in agriculture. While they stop pests from eating or destroying crops or causing harm to livestock, they can also cause terrible damage to ecosystems because they get ingested by worms, insects, and plants, thus endangering the balance of nature.

## WHY IS IT CAUSING EXTINCTION?

In the case of bees, pesticides are causing their numbers to decline rapidly because they either kill the bees when they land on flowers or kill the colony when the bee returns home to the hive.

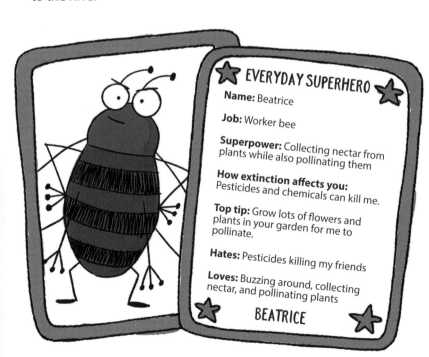

⭐ EVERYDAY SUPERHERO ⭐

**Name:** Beatrice

**Job:** Worker bee

**Superpower:** Collecting nectar from plants while also pollinating them

**How extinction affects you:** Pesticides and chemicals can kill me.

**Top tip:** Grow lots of flowers and plants in your garden for me to pollinate.

**Hates:** Pesticides killing my friends

**Loves:** Buzzing around, collecting nectar, and pollinating plants

BEATRICE

## OVERFISHING

Do you love eating fish? Me too. But unfortunately, certain bad fishing practices are having a terrible effect on some fish populations.

We have been eating fish for thousands of years. If we fish sensibly and don't take too much, it's fine. However, when we take too much, it's known as overfishing. That's when we create problems.

## WHY IS IT CAUSING EXTINCTION?

Some fishing practices are OK because they leave plenty of fish in the sea. But when too many fish are taken, fish populations can decline too fast for nature to keep up. If young fish are taken, then there will be fewer adult fish to reproduce. In some cases, nets and lines catch other species—this is known as bycatch—and this can have a terrible effect on those species' populations too.

Time to call time-out on eating shrimp!

**IMPORTANT NEWS!**
In fisheries where they use huge nets to catch shrimp, they also catch other fish accidentally. What a waste!

## POACHING AND TRAFFICKING FOR TREATING AILMENTS

Some people believe that parts of some animals can have health benefits if they use them as medicine.

The best-known example of this is the rhino. Although there are no proven medical benefits, some believe that consuming ground rhino horn can cure all kinds of diseases.

## WHY IS IT CAUSING EXTINCTION?

When animal products are used to treat ailments, it means they have a value. The more people poach an animal, the more it is later protected by law, then the more it is worth, and the more likely it is that the animals will face extinction because of this cycle.

### IMPORTANT NEWS!

The pangolin is the most poached and trafficked animal on Earth. It is protected under international law, but it is estimated that more than one million of them were poached and sold in a ten-year period. Their scales are used in East and Southeast Asian medicine, even though there is no evidence to suggest that they have any healing properties.

43

## INVASIVE SPECIES

Ever since humans began traveling around the world, they brought animals, plants, and diseases with them, whether they meant to or not. Sometimes they brought animals to act as pest control or to make life easier for themselves.

In the 1840s, camels were imported to Australia as pack animals (to carry stuff). Once they were not needed anymore, they were set free. Now there are about a million of them living wild. The camels don't belong there and haven't evolved there, making life difficult for some of the native animals.

## WHY IS IT CAUSING EXTINCTION?

While invasive species often adapt well to their new environments, they put enormous pressure on native species, often sending them into decline. The gray squirrel is a perfect example. It was imported to the UK in the 1870s from the US. They brought with them a disease called the squirrel parapoxvirus, which is very dangerous to UK-native red squirrels. As a result, and also because of the gray's success, the red squirrel has been displaced in most of the UK and is endangered.

### SURPRISING NEWS!
In the UK, the red squirrel's archenemy, the pine marten, is also endangered. But it has been discovered that pine martens find it easier to kill and eat gray squirrels than red squirrels. So where you find them, you are likely to find red squirrels too!

## FARMING

Food production has had a huge effect on the planet. Even though about half the world's habitable land is used for farming, hunger still affects about 10 percent of the world's population.

Farmers are also producing more of the same crops around the world and using practices that exclude biodiversity because they devote vast tracts of land to one crop.

## WHY IS IT CAUSING EXTINCTION?

One of the problems with global food production is that as more popular types of foods take over farmland, it can push out traditional local varieties of fruit, vegetables, and grains, which then become scarce.

On another level, farming single crops in large areas, with bigger fields and fewer trees and bushes, means that mammals, birds, flowers, and native plants have nowhere to live. Crops don't provide food for many animals, which means animals that rely on native plants go hungry.

Soil health is important too. When land is plowed, it can lose its nutrients and the bacteria that live in the soil through erosion. This means the soil isn't as healthy, which means more and more fertilizer is put on it. This endangers animals and plants that live nearby.

# THE PLANET IN THE BALANCE

Now that you've gotten a grip on extinction and what it means, your next mission is to learn to appreciate nature, how we are connected to it, and how it supports us every day. This mission is super easy and lots of fun, and I hope you'll really enjoy it. And, in doing it, you might just help to save a few animals and plants too.

## ABOUT ECOSYSTEMS

The natural world is made up of thousands of ecosystems, communities of interconnected and interacting organisms, each of which supports life. Some ecosystems can be as big as the Amazon rainforest, with millions of plants, animals, fish, and insects relying on each other for food, shelter, and nutrients. Others can be as small as a garden pond. Ecosystems can be underwater, up a tree, or under a log and can cover a huge area or can take up just a tiny space.

### QUICK QUIZ
Q: What's the world's biggest ecosystem?

ANSWER: The ocean!

**YOUR 2-MINUTE MISSION**: **Make a terrarium. It is a self-sustaining ecosystem. It's pretty easy to make one, although you might need some help from an adult.**
**15 POINTS**

**PLANT POWER**: Plants make oxygen in the daytime by taking on carbon dioxide and water and using sunlight to turn it into carbon, which is new growth. At night they respire, giving out water and nutrients.

**YOU WILL NEED**:
A large glass jar that can be sealed;
gravel; some activated charcoal;
compost or soil; water; plants, like ferns

1. Place the gravel in the bottom of the jar.
2. Add the activated charcoal.
3. Place the compost or soil on top.
4. Plant the fern.
5. Put some water in the bottom of the jar, then seal it.
6. Place the jar in a sunny spot and keep an eye on it.
   In time it should be self-sustaining because it has
   everything it needs: light, water, carbon dioxide.

## FOOD CHAINS AND FOOD WEBS

Within every ecosystem there will be a food chain. It's called a chain because all the links in it are essential, and if one link breaks, the whole chain falls apart.

If one part of the chain goes extinct—perhaps because humans have damaged their nest sites—then the balance is lost and the food chain is broken.

When all the food chains in an ecosystem are joined together, they form a food web. Food webs look more complex, but they are basically lots of chains connected together.

This is the way animals provide food for each other and how they benefit the ecosystem as a whole, because everything in that ecosystem is important. It's easiest to explain when we talk about the sea.

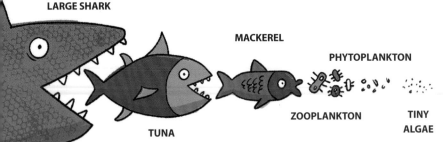

**LARGE SHARK**
**MACKEREL**
**PHYTOPLANKTON**
**ZOOPLANKTON**
**TINY ALGAE**
**TUNA**

## PRODUCERS, CONSUMERS, AND DECOMPOSERS

A food chain always starts with a producer, an organism that makes food. This is usually a green plant, because plants can make their own food by photosynthesis using energy from the Sun. A food chain ends with a consumer, an animal, such as a toothy shark, that eats another animal or a plant. But no food chain would be complete without a decomposer, which turns organic waste, like decaying plants, into inorganic material, such as soil.

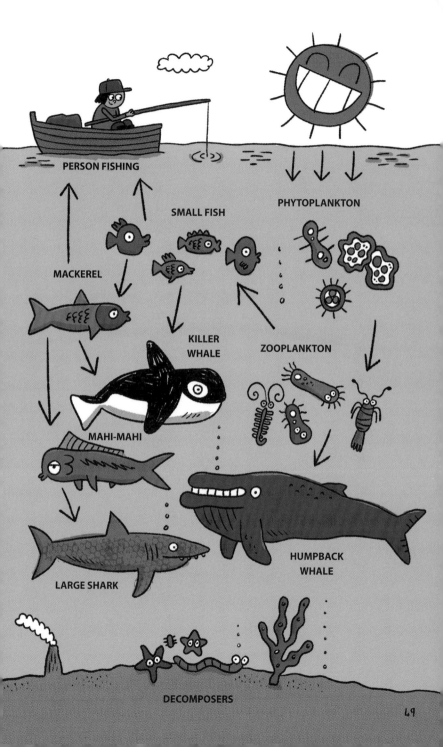

PERSON FISHING

SMALL FISH

PHYTOPLANKTON

MACKEREL

KILLER
WHALE

ZOOPLANKTON

MAHI-MAHI

LARGE SHARK

HUMPBACK
WHALE

DECOMPOSERS

49

## KEYSTONE SPECIES

Sharks are apex predators, which means they are at the top of the food chain. They are also keystone species, which means they are vitally important to keep the ecosystem in balance. Sharks help to keep the larger fish healthy and in check (sharks are lazy and often prefer to eat weak or injured fish) with the number of smaller fish below them in the food chain.

If you lose the sharks you lose the balance, which will change the ecosystem. It's also important to remember that each link in the food chain—I cannot emphasize this enough—is vitally important. Even the little guys—the plankton and the small fry—are essential for life on Earth. And if we lose any one of them, we lose everything.

YOUR 2-MINUTE MISSION: **Draw your own food chain. It could be real or imagined, and it will help you understand the link between one animal and the next. What will eat what? Are they dinosaurs? Elephants? Sharks? Dolphins? GO WILD! 5 POINTS**

## WHY YOU MATTER

You are important because you have some control over how you live. Whenever you make a decision to look after nature or to destroy it—to let the lawn grow wild or to mow it, for example—you have an effect on nature.

Everything you do is important. It really is. And the sooner you realize that, the sooner you'll be able to take your place on the superhero podium as an extinction-fighting wonder kid with a big heart and a love of nature who is superstrong and kind to animals. What more could you want to be?

51

# FIGHT EXTINCTION FROM THE GROUND UP

Now that you've read the first few chapters of this book, you should realize that extinction is a big problem all over the planet. You might also think that there's not much you can do for animals that are in danger in other parts of the world or that are struggling with problems that seem really big.

While you will probably grow up to be an awesome superhero and will be able to do this when you are older, you need to think about what you can do at home, right here, right now.

Let's start at ground level, with the little guys. I'm talking about the creepy-crawlies. They need your help!

## WHAT ARE CREEPY-CRAWLIES?

Creepy-crawlies are all those little things that creep and crawl (obviously). They include insects, spiders, centipedes, snails, beetles, and worms. They are usually known, collectively, as invertebrates, which means they don't have a spine (or backbone). And these are divided into those that have legs and those that don't. Some of them are beyond belief. Some are so small you can hardly see them. Some are beautiful. All of them are amazing.

## BE A FRIEND TO CREEPY-CRAWLIES

Even if creepy-crawlies scare you, I'd like you to at least begin to try to understand how wonderful, different, wild, and amazing they are. Make friends with them. Let them have their space and don't get too close if you don't want to. Just don't step on them! We need them as much as they need us to look after them. It's that simple. Let's get to work!

**YOUR 2-MINUTE MISSION:** Go outside and see if you can find any creepy-crawlies. Don't get too close or touch them. Replace any stones carefully and try not to harm any of your creepy-crawly friends. **10 POINTS**

**FEARFUL FACT:** Are you terrified of centipedes? Freaked out by flies? Spooked by spiders? It could be that you have entomophobia, a fear of insects.

**YOU WILL NEED:**
- An open mind
- Some outdoor space
- A magnifying glass
- A notepad
- A smartphone
- Maybe also some kneepads

### ⭐ EVERYDAY SUPERHERO ⭐

**Name:** Stephen

**Job:** Stag beetle

**Superpower:** I have huge antlers.

**How extinction affects you:**
My home and food source are being destroyed.

**Top tip:** Make sure you have lots of dead and rotting wood in your garden. Stag beetles love it!

**Hates:** Not being able to find somewhere to pupate underground

**Loves:** Wrestling with my big antlers!

⭐ **STEPHEN** ⭐

**FACT:** There are at least twenty-four different stag beetle species in the United States!

**YOUR 2-MINUTE MISSION:** Get to know your creepy-crawlies better. Books can help you identify insects. Apps are great at helping you find out what they do and how they act. (Beware: some may have in-app purchases.) **5 POINTS**

**CREEPY-CRAWLY FACT:** Scientists have found around a million insect species. Incredibly, scientists estimate that there are anywhere from two to thirty million species yet to be named!

## WHY ARE CREEPY-CRAWLIES IMPORTANT?

Invertebrates are vital to life on Earth. They live everywhere—in your house, in the garden, in the fields, and in the oceans. They provide food for larger animals and birds, act as pollinators (which means they fertilize plants), and also serve as nature's great recyclers, turning dead plants and animals into healthy, life-giving soil. If the invertebrates go, we won't be able to grow crops, won't have healthy soil, and will also lose lots more of the birds and animals that rely on them for food.

## THE UNKNOWN APOCALYPSE

It's easy to understand the extinction of big animals like elephants, but it's a lot harder to get a grip on insects—partly because we don't know so much about them but also because it's hard to count them. We don't know how many have gone, but a 2018 study estimated that we have lost about 60 percent of the world's population of invertebrates since the 1970s.

# WHY ARE CREEPY-CRAWLIES FACING EXTINCTION?

**HABITAT LOSS:** Invertebrates are under threat because of habitat loss where forests are felled and agricultural land is expanded.

**POLLUTION:** Pollution from factories, industry, and vehicles is also another risk to invertebrates.

**CLIMATE CHANGE:** Adverse weather, warming seas, and changing seasonal averages can cause terrible problems for some insect populations and the invertebrates that make up 92 percent of all ocean life.

**PESTICIDES:** Lots of insects and invertebrates are viewed as parasites and pests by the farming industry because they can destroy food crops. As a result, we have invented pesticides and chemicals that kill creepy-crawlies by the millions.

YOUR 2-MINUTE MISSION: **Weed killer is terrible for insects and invertebrates. Ask your caregivers, school, and town to stop using it, if they do. You can write letters and emails or even start a protest. 10 POINTS**

CREEPY-CRAWLY FACT: People who study insects are called entomologists. What does that make you, as someone who saves them? A superhero entomologist, of course!

You superhero bug lover, you!

YOUR 2-MINUTE MISSION: Name your pet spider. Spiders are great. So next time you find one, don't harm it. Give it a name, let it do its thing, and be its friend. 10 POINTS

YOUR 2-MINUTE MISSION: Inspire your friends to take care of insects too. Could you dress up like an insect? Or maybe you could write a story about your pet spider? 10 POINTS

WEBBY TIP: House spiders, funnily enough, only live inside houses, which means they don't survive outside. They are largely harmless to us and help by eating flies and insects that come inside.

# FIGHT EXTINCTION IN THE GARDEN

Do you have a garden? If you do, then great, this chapter is for you. But even if you only have a little outside space—a balcony or a small yard—then it's still possible to fight extinction with that too. That's because everything you do makes a difference. I know I keep telling you this, but it's important for you to remember that you are important, you matter, and the things you do have an effect on the planet and all the animals in it. Even if it's just something tiny, it still counts.

## NATURE WILL FIND A WAY

Nature is incredible. Somehow it will find a way to inhabit your spaces, whether you like it or not! Notice how plants grow in between the cracks in the sidewalk or how adults get annoyed by "weeds" growing everywhere. Once nature gets in, it's difficult to keep it down—and that's fantastic.

YOUR 2-MINUTE MISSION: Can you see plants growing in the cracks in the sidewalk, in gaps between bricks, and in spaces that are unloved or forgotten? Isn't it amazing how nature always seems to find a way to grow—no matter how hard we make it! 5 POINTS

# BEWARE THE INVADERS!

Sometimes nature has a habit of going a bit wild and taking over, especially when it comes to plants and animals that aren't supposed to be there. Invasive species—which are from other countries or continents brought here accidentally or on purpose—are like uninvited party guests. They crash an event they weren't invited to and just do what they want, when they want. What it means is that native plants find it hard to find their space—in fact, it's been completely taken over! This can lead to local plants and wildlife struggling to survive.

## GET TO KNOW THE BAD GUYS!

**Japanese knotweed:**
Pointed leaves. Red stems in spring. Looks a bit like bamboo. Grows up to 8 inches (20 centimeters) per day.

**Himalayan balsam:**
Long, pointed leaves with serrated edges. Flowers can be white, pink, or purple with hanging green seed pods. Produces lots of nectar so bees love it and ignore other plants.

**Creeping Bellflower:**
Comes up in spring. Looks a bit like a bluebell, but the flowers come in colors from blue to blue-violet. It can have up to fifteen thousand seeds per plant!

**YOUR 2-MINUTE MISSION:** Take this book outside and see if you can spot any invasive species. If it's Japanese knotweed, you'll need to tell an adult. It is on the National Park Service's Targeted Plant Species Watchlist, and eradicating it requires special techniques.
**10 POINTS**

# FLOWERS WITHOUT LOVE. WHY WEEDS ARE ADORABLE!

Did you know that weeds are just plants that get a bad rap? It's true. Lots of people believe some plants are simply weeds and remove them from their gardens. It's incredibly sad! Lots of these misunderstood plants are AMAZING for wildlife because of the food they provide for the birds and insects and the pollen they produce for bees.

Some weeds are invasive and spread quickly, which means they aren't good for native birds and insects, but others can be fantastic and help your garden or outdoor space.

**YOUR 2-MINUTE MISSION: Download a plant identification app. Then go out into the garden or park and try to identify a few plants. Are they considered weeds? Are they friend or foe? You decide, based on how you think they help the natural world. 10 POINTS**

## SOME FRIENDLY WEEDS

**Daisy:**
Lovely white flowers that many consider a weed. But pollinating insects—and birds—love them!

**White clover:**
This little plant is great for everyone as it is good for the soil and creepy-crawlies. And that's food for the birds.

**Dandelion:**
When bumblebees come out of hibernation in spring, dandelions are often the first thing they seek because they are the first flowers to bloom.

# BE KIND TO BEES

They might be small, but bees are mighty. They are pollinators, which means that they are vital when it comes to helping plants produce fruit. Sound complicated? Sorry. Let me explain. Bees love the nectar and pollen produced by flowers. They visit lots of them, collecting nectar either for themselves or for their hives.

When they do this, they carry pollen on the hairs of their bodies to other plants of the same species. These bits of pollen then rub off on the reproductive parts of the new plants and fertilize them. Once this has happened, the plant can grow fruit and the plant's life cycle can continue.

## UN-BEE-LIEVABLE FACTS:

♠ There are thousands of bee species around the world. Many of them are specialists and have adapted to pollinate certain plants. If those bees die, the plants would die too.
♠ Bees are vital to us because they pollinate crops we need for food. Honeybees alone pollinate more than 130 types of fruit and vegetables. Without them, we'd go hungry.
♠ Humans also cultivate bees for their honey and the wax they make in their hives. Without them, no honey!

YOUR 2-MINUTE MISSION: In the autumn, plant a bee-friendly flowerpot with bulbs of crocus, snowdrop, grape hyacinth, and scented daffodil. The bulbs will produce flowers in the spring when the bees need them most. 30 POINTS

# WHY BEES ARE THREATENED WITH EXTINCTION

All kinds of bees—from honeybees to solitary bees and bumblebees—are under threat. Globally, it is estimated that 40 percent of all bee species are in danger of extinction. The reasons are numerous but include the loss of habitats that bees love (when we build houses or farms on wildflower meadows, that takes away food from the bees!), the use of insecticides and herbicides (harmful chemicals that kill insect pests also kill bees), climate change (bees can be confused by seasons changing early or late and their favorite flowers blooming at the wrong time), invasive species, and disease (such as deformed wing virus, which can impact a bee's ability to fly).

**YOUR 2-MINUTE MISSION: Make a bee hotel. 50 POINTS**

### YOU WILL NEED:

A two-liter plastic soda bottle with the top cut off; several lengths of bamboo in different diameters; some biodegradable string

1. Choose pieces of bamboo with single or no knots.
2. Fill the bottle with the lengths of bamboo, adding enough so they don't fall out and so that the soda bottle overhangs the ends of the bamboo about a half an inch. Insert the string in the bottle so it comes out both ends and there is enough string to hang the bee hotel up or fasten it to a safe location.
3. Place in the garden somewhere sunny and about 3 feet (1 meter) off the ground. Leave alone. In the spring, the bees will find your hotel and lay their eggs. The following year, the new bees will emerge!

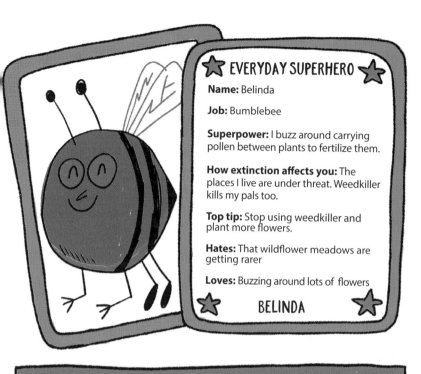

### ★ EVERYDAY SUPERHERO ★

**Name:** Belinda

**Job:** Bumblebee

**Superpower:** I buzz around carrying pollen between plants to fertilize them.

**How extinction affects you:** The places I live are under threat. Weedkiller kills my pals too.

**Top tip:** Stop using weedkiller and plant more flowers.

**Hates:** That wildflower meadows are getting rarer

**Loves:** Buzzing around lots of flowers

★ **BELINDA** ★

**YOUR 2-MINUTE MISSION:** Let dandelions grow in your garden. Dandelions are among the first flowers to bloom in spring. That means bees can feast on nectar soon after a long winter or hibernation. **10 POINTS**

## LOVE YOUR LAWN

Did you know that your lawn may well be one of the greatest tools you have in your battle to fight extinction? Yes! Lawns are places that can either be without much life and biodiversity or be full of wildlife, flowers, and, under the surface, worms, grubs, and insects. Grass that isn't cut too short and is left to grow longer between cuts is better for the planet and a great way to help fight extinction from your own backyard!

## WHAT'S THE PROBLEM WITH LAWNS?

When lawns are cut short, free of weeds, and treated with pesticides and lawn treatments, they are like green deserts because they don't provide much of a home for wildlife, insects, or grubs and snails. They might look neat and tidy, but they can't support a huge amount of biodiversity—something we now know is vital for nature to thrive.

YOUR 2-MINUTE MISSION: **Talk to the mower in your family about mowing every three weeks instead of every week. 10 POINTS**

SAY SO LONG TO SHORTER LAWNS!

**YOUR 2-MINUTE MISSION:** Want to earn some money and help save the planet? Offer to mow the lawn! If you raise the cutting blades to their maximum height (get an adult to help with this), it will help insects and birds.
**20 POINTS**

## YOUR LOCAL LAWNS

Even if you don't have a lawn at home, you can make changes to the green areas on your street or in your town. You can do this by writing to your local government to ask them to consider letting the grass on medians and in parks grow longer than usual or to replace some grass with local wildflowers and other beneficial plants.

You could also ask people on your street to let the grass grow longer too. Some of them might change their habits when you point out the advantages of a longer, greener lawn.

**YOUR 2-MINUTE MISSION:** Make a flyer to put in the mailboxes on your street asking people to reduce their mowing from once a week to once every three weeks. Make it colorful and don't forget to include facts from this book. **10 POINTS**

**FACT:** Researchers found that mowing lawns less often increases biodiversity, saves money, and reduces weeds!

## MISSION 6

# FIGHT EXTINCTION AT THE BIRDFEEDER

Recently, scientists reported that 49 percent of the world's eleven thousand bird species are in decline, and one in eight bird species is threatened with global extinction. It is estimated that the US and Canada alone have lost around three billion birds since the 1970s. Even sparrows and finches have seen declines over the past few decades. Imagine not seeing them in your yard! It's unthinkable. Isn't it?

There are lots of reasons why birds are endangered. Listing them reads like a history of humankind, unfortunately, as more often than not they are due to us. Of course, the good news is that it means we can stop the decline if we act together and quickly.

⭐ **EVERYDAY SUPERHERO** ⭐

**Name:** Kaia

**Job:** North Island brown kiwi

**Superpower:** I am so rare that there were only seventy thousand of my kind left about thirty years ago.

**How extinction affects you:** My eggs were getting eaten by invasive species such as stoats.

**Top tip:** Support kiwi rescue charities

**Hates:** Dogs that chase me

**Loves:** The New Zealand rainforest

KAIA

# WHAT CAUSES BIRDS TO GO EXTINCT?

**INVASIVE SPECIES:**
Some birds are extremely vulnerable
to invasive species. Birds, like the
gorgeous but very flightless kākāpō,
are especially vulnerable, because
invasive species such as stoats and
rats make easy prey of them.

**LOSS OF HABITAT:**
All over the world bird habitats are being
lost to human development or agriculture,
leaving many birds with nowhere to live. The
UK tree sparrow population has declined by
95 percent due to the loss of hedgerows and
more aggressive farming practices.

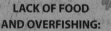

**LACK OF FOOD
AND OVERFISHING:**
Atlantic puffins are endangered
because warming seas and
overfishing have reduced the number
of fish in their habitat, leaving them
hungry and at risk.

**CHEMICALS AND POLLUTANTS:**
When birds eat food that is
contaminated with chemicals, those
chemicals can build up in their bodies
and eventually kill them. The California
condor frequently eats game that has
been shot. Consuming the bullets puts
them at risk for lead poisoning.

## HOW TO HELP THE BIRDS IN YOUR BACKYARD

Lots of birds live among us in towns, cities, and in the countryside. In difficult times—the winter or early spring—they can sometimes struggle to find food. For many birds, the threats they face are due to lack of food because of declining habitats.

You might think that birds should be able to survive losing their habitats, wouldn't you? After all, most birds can fly. The problem, however, is when the habitat provides food that can't be found anywhere else. If a bird is specialized or needs a special kind of food—that exists in only one habitat—then the loss of that habitat will inevitably mean food is more scarce and survival is harder for the birds.

**YOUR 2-MINUTE MISSION: Make a seed cake for the birds to eat! It's really easy (but you might need to get a little help from one of your pet adults). 30 POINTS**

### YOU WILL NEED:

½ cup lard; 1 cup birdseed; ½ cup sunflower seeds; ¼ cup dried fruit; ¼ cup cornmeal; 4–6 clean plastic yogurt cups

1. In a pan, melt ½ cup of lard at medium-low heat.
2. Remove from heat and add in 1 cup of birdseed, ½ cup of sunflower seeds, ¼ cup of dried fruit, and ¼ cup of cornmeal.
3. When it has cooled a bit, but before it sets, pour the mixture into a few clean plastic yogurt cups.
4. When the cakes have set, push them out of the cups and put them (one at a time) on your bird café or in your birdfeeder.

**YOUR 2-MINUTE MISSION: Make a bird café. It can be as simple as hanging seed cakes off a hook on your balcony. But if you have help and a few bits of wood, it's easy. 50 POINTS**

### YOU WILL NEED:

A 4-foot-long (a little over 1-meter-long) piece of wood; a board 12 inches (30 centimeters) square; four small pieces of wood ½ inch (1 centimeter) high; screws; wood glue; hooks; a drill

1. Find a length of wood about 4 feet (a little over 1 meter) tall. At least one end should be flat. Dig a hole and plant it so it's upright with at least 3 feet (1 meter) of the flat end of the wood sticking out of the ground.
2. Find a board that is about 12 inches (30 centimeters) square. Use screws or wood glue to attach a wooden rim around the edges of the board at least ½ inch (1 centimeter) high so all the birdseed does not fall out, but leave gaps at the corners for easier cleaning.
3. Screw the board to the upright piece of wood to create a platform for the birds. If your platform needs more support, screw at least two smaller pieces of wood to the upright plank and the platform.
4. Place your seed cake on the board or screw hooks underneath the board so you can hang seed cakes or feeders from them. Ta-da! A bird café!

**YOUR 2-MINUTE MISSION: Take a book out of the library or download an app and learn to identify the birds that visit your bird café. 10 POINTS**

# FIGHT EXTINCTION WITH WATER

We take water for granted, don't we? I know I do. It comes out of my tap and falls from the sky above my house. When I hear about animals losing their fight with extinction, water leaks from my eyes too.

It's simple. Water is life and without it we would all perish. We need it to drink, to wash, to cook. Nature needs water too. Plants need it to grow, animals need it to drink and wash. Insects need it for their life cycle. Amphibians need it to lay their eggs. Fish need it to live in!

It seems, sometimes, like there is water everywhere. And if there is, why do we need to use it to help fight extinction?

## WHY SAVING WATER IS IMPORTANT

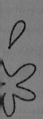

There are lots of reasons why it's important we don't waste water. First, water from the tap costs money, so the less you use, the less your parents or caregivers have to pay.

Second, water requires energy and effort to be filtered and pumped to your house, so it saves carbon (and helps fight climate change) when you use less. The less water you use at home, the less water has to be taken out of nature (rivers, reservoirs, and lakes) and the more there is for animals and plants.

Third, think again about watering with tap water. Nature doesn't always like the water we drink and prefers rainwater. That's because water from our taps sometimes has too many added chemicals for many plants and creatures.

## SAVING RAINWATER

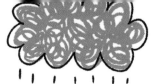

Are you growing plants or vegetables? If you are, then in order for them to survive, they will need to be watered by natural rainfall and/or by you. Instead of giving them water from the tap, it's much better to give them rainwater you have collected. It's cheaper too.

**YOUR 2-MINUTE MISSION: Harvesting rainwater is really easy to do. Put out a bucket on your windowsill, on the balcony, or in your backyard, and see how much water you collect when it rains. Save it and use it to water your plants, either indoors or outdoors, when they need it. 10 POINTS**

## HARVESTING MORE THAN JUST A BUCKET

The bigger the area you can collect water from, the more water you'll be able to harvest. Rainwater that runs off the roof and down to the yard or sidewalk is an excellent place to start. Putting a bucket or a big container like a water barrel underneath a drainpipe can collect lots of water very quickly. It's not that easy to set up, so you will have to talk to your parents or caregivers. Try to explain that it will help save money.

**YOUR 2-MINUTE MISSION: Speak to your parents or caregivers about setting up a water barrel. If you grow plants, it will be useful for watering them. 10 POINTS**

# WHY PONDS ARE AMAZING

Ponds are incredible mini ecosystems that can support all kinds of plants, insects, animals, and birds. They can be big or they can be tiny. Even the smallest ponds can attract insects and amphibians and become little worlds in themselves that are self-sufficient and don't need much looking after. They become homes for insects that need water for their life cycle and provide a nursery for animals that need it to breed. Ponds can also help support lots of life around them by providing food.

## AT RISK!

According to scientists, around 33 percent of all aquatic insects are in danger of extinction, including the caddis fly.

## ⭐ EVERYDAY SUPERHERO ⭐

**Name:** Claire

**Job:** Caddis fly

**Superpower:** I live as a larva and cover myself in a protective suit of stones and pebbles.

**How extinction affects you:** We are losing our homes too, and without water we won't survive.

**Top tip:** Make us a pond!

**Hates:** That ponds are disappearing

**Loves:** Living in your little pond, safe from harm, getting ready to fly away!

### CLAIRE

# MAKE YOUR OWN POND!

Making a pond can be really simple. The simplest ponds are just containers with rainwater (that you have saved). Even if you don't have a backyard, you could still talk to your teacher about making a pond at school. Explain to your classmates why it's important and ask them to help. It would be a great project!

YOUR 2-MINUTE MISSION: **Make a simple pond by using an old bowl. 10 POINTS**

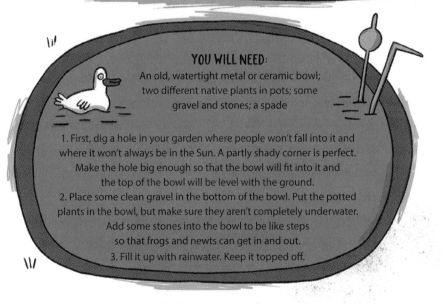

### YOU WILL NEED:
An old, watertight metal or ceramic bowl; two different native plants in pots; some gravel and stones; a spade

1. First, dig a hole in your garden where people won't fall into it and where it won't always be in the Sun. A partly shady corner is perfect. Make the hole big enough so that the bowl will fit into it and the top of the bowl will be level with the ground.
2. Place some clean gravel in the bottom of the bowl. Put the potted plants in the bowl, but make sure they aren't completely underwater. Add some stones into the bowl to be like steps so that frogs and newts can get in and out.
3. Fill it up with rainwater. Keep it topped off.

# WHAT WILL YOU FIND IN YOUR POND?

Wait and see what arrives in your pond. Your pond might take a little time to get established. But that's OK. It may take a few weeks for insects and amphibians to find it. Keep looking, though, and see what you find.

# FIGHT EXTINCTION IN THE SUPERMARKET

You might not expect to see many animals in the supermarket. In fact, you may not see any animals at all when you go shopping. Can you imagine an orangutan swinging from the ceiling in the cereal aisle? I thought not.

But, believe it or not, you can help orangutans—and a whole lot of other plants and animals—by helping with the shopping. When you help out at the supermarket, or better still, at your local shops, you'll be able to influence the choices your family makes and that could, in turn, help nature.

In some ways, the way your family shops might well be one of the most powerful tools you have in your fight against extinction.

Let me explain.

## HOW CAN YOUR SHOPPING AFFECT EXTINCTION?

All our food has to be grown or caught. From cornflakes to sustainable salmon, everything has a story: where and how it's grown, how it's caught or pastured on a farm, how it's treated while it's growing, and where it has come from to get to you. This story is vitally important when it comes to extinction.

# THE STORY OF YOUR FOOD

Do you know where your food comes from? Which of the following do you think is best for nature?

**COW 1: Reared on land created by cutting down rainforests**

**COW 2: Reared on a factory farm in the US and fed GMO soybeans from Brazil**

Meat is shipped to the supermarket by boat or plane.

Meat travels to the supermarket in big trucks.

Meat is sold at your local farmers' market.

**COW 3: Reared on a farm in the US and fed on a wildflower meadow, outside**

## HOW MUCH?

When it comes to budgeting, eating "sustainable" food presents difficult choices because it is often more expensive. So don't put pressure on your parents or caregivers to buy organic food if it isn't in their budget. That's not fair to them. However, what you can do is learn to cook with fresh ingredients and fruit and veggies, which can be really cheap and will help you in your mission to fight extinction. Find out more in Mission 9.

FISH
EGGS
APPLES
BREAD

**YOUR 2-MINUTE MISSION:**
**Find a food that your family eats regularly. Check out the ingredients. If it has GMOs or palm oil in it, find an alternative, if you can. Do a price comparison. Is it cheaper or more expensive? 10 POINTS**

## WHEN FOOD CAUSES EXTINCTIONS

In some parts of the world, forest is cleared to make way for agriculture and for rearing livestock. This is having a devastating effect on nature because it deprives all the native species of a home, forcing them into smaller and smaller pockets of forest.

**SAY GOODBYE TO THE JUNGLE:** Since 2016, an average of 69 million acres of forests have been cut down every year. That's one soccer field of forest lost every single second of the day.

Even in the US our food production is causing extinctions. Pesticides are polluting our rivers and soil, and habitats are being torn up to make bigger and bigger fields of single crops. This results in a loss of biodiversity as native animals and plants have nowhere to live and no food.

**ADIEU TO THE MEADOWS:** In 2020, 1.8 million acres (7,284 square kilometers) of grassland habitat in the US and Canada were plowed for farmland. Grasslands are vital for the health of songbirds and other wildlife species in the Great Plains.

When it comes to food caught in the sea, it's a similar problem. Nets used to target one species of fish often catch lots of other fish along the way, including dolphins, whales, and other animals at risk of extinction. This is known as bycatch.

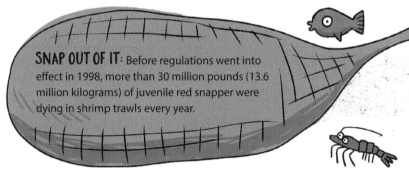

**SNAP OUT OF IT:** Before regulations went into effect in 1998, more than 30 million pounds (13.6 million kilograms) of juvenile red snapper were dying in shrimp trawls every year.

Also, lots of smaller species of fish are targeted to make food for farmed salmon. Farmed salmon takes about 3.3 pounds (1.5 kilograms) of fish to grow 2.2 pounds (1 kilogram) of meat. That's unsustainable, isn't it? Farming salmon has a bad effect on local wildlife because of disease and pollution. Overfishing also steals food from seabirds and fish, driving them closer to extinction.

## WHEN SCIENCE ALSO CAUSES EXTINCTIONS

Humans have been working for years to "design" crops that are resistant to drought and disease. These are known as genetically modified organisms (GMOs). It makes sense if we can grow more to feed all eight billion of us, right? Well, yes. It does.

But some companies modify crops for profit and to control the market. They sell seeds that have been modified to be pesticide resistant, which means that farmers can use pesticides on crops without killing them. The pesticides will kill pests and, sadly, pollinators, like bees and other insects. These pesticides can accumulate in the ground and ruin the health of the soil, killing worms and other invertebrates in the process.

Another problem with GMO crops is that seed companies make farmers sign an agreement to purchase new seed each year, rather than saving seeds from their crops to plant the following year. This costs farmers money and means that local varieties of the crops die out because all the crops are the same.

YOUR 2-MINUTE MISSION: Add organic material, such as compost, to your garden. Worms are the heroes of the mud. They recycle dead matter—like leaves and dead flowers— and turn it into healthy, nutrient-rich soil that's great for growing. 20 POINTS

## WHAT DOES ALL THIS MEAN?

Our shopping is vital in the fight against extinction. If we make good choices, then we can support positive and sustainable food production. If we make bad choices—buying GMO foods or products that are grown on rainforest land or reared unsustainably—we aren't helping at all. Who'd have thought your shopping could be so important!

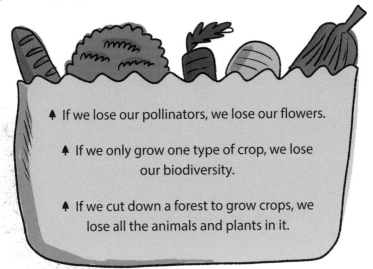

♠ If we lose our pollinators, we lose our flowers.

♠ If we only grow one type of crop, we lose our biodiversity.

♠ If we cut down a forest to grow crops, we lose all the animals and plants in it.

## WHAT CAN YOU DO ABOUT IT?

It's all about choices. The choices you make now may help to define the future of lots of plants, animals, insects, and ecosystems. Buying fresh, seasonal, and local ingredients is the very best way to fight extinction. Buying from local shops, butchers, seafood markets, and farmers' markets is by far the best way to do this. It can be more fun too. You get to meet nice people, talk about where food comes from, and maybe even learn some fun new recipes.

## LOOK AT THE LABELS

The labels on food can tell you a lot of stuff, from the calories to sugar and protein content. By law, labels have to say whether a product contains ingredients that are genetically modified. And they should tell you the country of origin too.

YOUR 2-MINUTE MISSION: **While you might not be able to change what food your family buys, you can look at the labels in your house. Check them out and see where your food comes from. Take a look at some of the ingredients you're consuming. 10 POINTS**

## SOY WHAT!

Soy is an ingredient that's in lots of food and that is used to feed livestock. It takes a lot of soybeans to raise cattle. Soy is grown all over the world, but most is produced in the US and Brazil. The rainforest and savannas in Brazil—important ecosystems for biodiversity—have been torn up for soy production. This means the local biodiversity is lost, animals lose their homes, many lose their food, and lots lose their lives, getting ever closer to extinction.

YOUR 2-MINUTE MISSION: **Check the labels of foods you suspect may have soy. If the soy is from Brazil, try to avoid it or find another option. 10 POINTS**

# PALMS OFF THE PALM OIL

Palm oil is another ingredient that is in a lot of foods, such as cereal, hot chocolate, chips, ice cream, and pizza. It's everywhere! The trouble is that there is such demand for it that rainforests are being cut down to grow it. This leaves lots of animals without homes or food. Orangutans are endangered particularly because of deforestation due to the spread of agriculture.

**YOUR 2-MINUTE MISSION:** Look at the labels on your groceries. See if you can spot the palm oil. 10 POINTS

## ⭐ EVERYDAY SUPERHERO ⭐

**Name:** Mubaraka

**Job:** Orangutan

**Superpower:** I have really long arms! The bigger males have arm spans of about 7 feet (2 meters)!

**How extinction affects you:** My home is being chopped down to grow palm oil.

**Top tip:** You can help me by not eating food with palm oil in it.

**Hates:** Seeing bulldozers in my forest

**Loves:** Living a quiet life in the trees with my kids and family

⭐ MUBARAKA ⭐

# FIGHT EXTINCTION IN THE KITCHEN

How's your cooking? Is it any good? Can you whip up a wicked lunch? I bet you can! If you can't, don't worry—you can learn. It's fun to cook, and it's great for you, the planet, and nature if you cook with fresh, local, and seasonal ingredients. And it'll be tastier too!

We already talked about going to the store and buying your food. Hopefully you've got a whole pile of super-fresh, local, and seasonal vegetables from your trip to the supermarket. Now what are you going to do with it?

## FUN FOODIE FACTS:

Kale is full of vitamins A and C, iron, and calcium, which means it is great for your hair! So eat it up!

Carrots contain retinol, a type of vitamin A, which can help you see better in low light! Amazing!

Broccoli contains more protein per calorie than steak—so give the beef a break. Yes! Munch on those tiny green trees!

Apples contain fructose, which is a natural sugar. So an apple in the morning will give you more sustained energy than a cup of coffee!

# ALL SUPERHEROES NEED SUPERFOODS!

We've already talked about why it's important to look at the ingredients in your food. So let's now look at the effect your diet can have on nature.

## EATING LOCALLY

The more you eat locally, the more you will be able to fight extinction. Native varieties of plants and animals have adapted to grow well where you are. Also, they provide food for, and support, insects and birds that are also suited for life near you.

**YOUR 2-MINUTE MISSION: Berries are grown all over the world. There are many varieties that are native to North America. See if you can find them in your local stores. 10 POINTS**

## ⭐ EVERYDAY SUPERHERO ⭐

**Name:** Benny

**Job:** Bristle-berry

**Superpower:** Not only do animals love me, but I also carry cultural significance to Indigenous people.

**How extinction affects you:** The bristle-berry habitat once covered a million acres across the Midwest! Now we grow almost exclusively in Minnesota's Anoka Sand Plain region.

**Top tip:** Look out for your own local berries and eat them when you can.

**Hates:** Land development and pollution

**Loves:** Growing in flat, sandy land

⭐ **BENNY** ⭐

## EATING FISH

Fish is a superfood, fit for all kinds of superheroes, but it can be problematic. We know that some methods of acquiring seafood, including shrimp and farmed salmon, aren't great for the planet and can contribute to the decline in biodiversity. But what about other types of fish?

The Monterey Bay Aquarium Seafood Watch program maintains a list to help you know if the fish you want to eat is OK or is being overfished. It's useful. However, the best way to acquire fish is to only buy sustainably caught fish, preferably from the ocean near where you live.

**YOUR 2-MINUTE MISSION:** Look at your favorite fish dish and then go and look it up at https://www.seafoodwatch.org/recommendations to see how your fish fared. Did it do OK? Great! Not so good? Maybe it's time to change brands or try something different. **20 POINTS**

## EATING MEAT

Some people don't eat meat because they believe that meat production is bad in all kinds of ways. But it's not always as straightforward as you might think. Yes, meat reared on factory farms and fed with soy grown on rainforest lands in Brazil isn't such a good choice. But buying meat that's been reared on natural grassland can be OK, if you are OK with eating animals.

The solution? Eating meat all the time is expensive and not so great for your health, so it's a good idea to limit your meat eating. Eat local, free-range, sustainably reared meat if you can.

# WHY VEGANISM CAN BE GOOD FOR THE PLANET

Being vegan means not eating any kind of animal product. That includes eggs, milk, meat, and fish. It can be a really healthy way to live as it means eating lots of vegetables. But it can bring its own challenges because it often results in eating food imported from the other side of the world—and that's bad for the climate. Veganism is VERY good if you eat local.

YOUR 2-MINUTE MISSION: **Go vegan for a day. I bet you'll find that you love being a plant-based superhero. If you like it, why not go vegan one day each week? 50 POINTS**

# EATING DAIRY

Drinking milk and eating cheese, yogurt, and butter can have a lot of health benefits. But dairy also comes with the problems of lost habitats, pollution, and less biodiversity. Tough choices!

YOUR 2-MINUTE MISSION: **Make oat milk and try it on your cereal. It's the very best milk for the planet. 40 POINTS**

### YOU WILL NEED:
1 cup of oats; 3 cups of water; a pinch of salt; a blender; muslin or a clean T-shirt

1. Add 1 cup of oats, 3 cups of fresh water, and a tiny pinch of salt to the blender. Whiz it up for 30–45 seconds, until it's all smooth.
2. Strain the milk through a muslin or clean T-shirt. You may need to strain more than once to remove excess starch. Drink! Do you like it?
3. For more ways to enjoy, try adding a pitted date, ½ teaspoon of vanilla, or even 2 tablespoons of cocoa powder (for chocolate oat milk)!

# FIGHT EXTINCTION IN THE BATHROOM

I know what you are thinking: What on Earth does my bathroom have to do with extinction?

Surprisingly, it does play a role!

That's because of the products that you might find in it.

From soaps, skin-care products, and shampoo to makeup, deodorant, and sunscreen, many of the products on the market contain palm oil.

Palm oil is good for moisturizing, cleansing, and conditioning, which is why so many companies use it. It's also cheap, which means it's good for their profits. Not so good for the planet, though.

Happily, some companies do make sustainable palm oil. They are usually marked with the Roundtable on Sustainable Palm Oil (RSPO) logo. It looks like this:

**FACT:** In the last twenty years, almost 80 percent of orangutans' natural habitat has been lost to palm oil plantations. And it's not just the orangutans. Millions of Indigenous people, who depend on the rainforest, have lost their forest homes too.

## CHEMICALS IN YOUR BATHROOM

Most bathroom products contain chemicals to clean our skin, teeth, and hair. The problem occurs when those products get flushed down the toilet or drain. They enter the sewage system and, eventually, flow into rivers and the sea.

Every drain in every house has a direct or indirect connection to bodies of water, even if they are hundreds of miles away. The trouble is that, even though water gets treated before it is cycled back to local bodies of water, some chemicals can still get through and cause harm to the environment. River systems— and all that lives in them—can be effectively destroyed because of pollution, although your shampoo is unlikely to have such a drastic effect. However, it all adds up, and the less we use harmful chemicals, the better.

THINK BEFORE YOU FLUSH!

## PLASTIC DANGER

Plastic that gets into the ocean, like cotton swabs or straws, can be a danger to wildlife, particularly sea turtles, almost all of which are endangered. Turtles mistake plastic bags for food, while seabirds mistake plastic fragments for fish. Plastic microbeads—tiny pieces of plastic in some beauty products—can also end up in the ocean, where they become toxic and harm fish and animals that eat them.

YOUR 2-MINUTE MISSION: **Visit a zero-waste store. They have lots of products that are plastic-free and good for the planet. Look for soap that doesn't contain palm oil and shampoo bars that you can rub on your head! 20 POINTS**

⭐ EVERYDAY SUPERHERO ⭐

**Name:** Larry

**Job:** Leatherback turtle

**Superpower:** I am huge! The biggest leatherback turtle ever recorded was almost 10 feet (3 meters) long!

**How extinction affects you:** I am in danger because of plastic bags and plastic pollution.

**Top tip:** Think about what products you use in the bathroom.

**Hates:** Plastic bags that look like jellyfish

**Loves:** Swimming in the open ocean

**LARRY**

**YOUR 2-MINUTE MISSION:** Done your missions? Good. Now it's time to have some superhero fun. Relax with an eco-friendly, homemade, luxury bath bomb. 50 POINTS

**Warning: Be careful when it comes to mixing the wet and dry ingredients—a bath bomb can go off at any moment! Get some help getting the ingredients together and take your time.**

## YOU WILL NEED:

1 cup baking soda; ½ cup citric acid; ½ cup cornstarch; ½ cup Epsom salt; 2 tablespoons olive oil; 2 teaspoons essential oil, such as lavender; a few drops of liquid food coloring; ¾ tablespoons water; a mixing bowl; a whisk; clean molds to shape your bath bombs

1. Wash and dry your hands. Put the baking soda, citric acid, cornstarch, and Epsom salt in a large mixing bowl, and stir it well.
2. Pour the olive oil, essential oil, and food coloring into another, smaller bowl. Mix together.
3. Very slowly add the oil mixture into the dry mixture a little at a time, and whisk between each addition. When it's all mixed together, add the water and stir it quickly to stop it from fizzing too much. CAREFUL. This is the important part. You need the mixture to clump together but not be too wet.
4. Press the mixture into your molds with your hands and then put in the fridge to dry and harden for at least twenty-four hours. Remove it from the mold, run the bath, and pop it in!
5. Dive in and watch it fizz.

# FIGHT EXTINCTION WITH YOUR MONEY

Sometimes, when the animals facing extinction are far away, struggling for survival in countries you may never see for yourself, it's difficult to fight for them directly. However, you can help the people who help them by supporting the work they do.

Giving money to charities that are involved in conservation work is a good way of helping animals that can't help themselves.

If you get an allowance, you could donate a part of it to conservation charities or save up to adopt an animal.

You could even start a fundraiser at school to help fund research and conservation efforts!

Imagine that! Your school could help save the life of a gorilla, an orangutan, or even a blue whale!

What amazing things you could do!

---

YOUR 2-MINUTE MISSION: Find an empty glass jar and a piece of recycled or reused paper. Write FOR FIGHTING EXTINCTION on the paper, and then use string or biodegradable tape to attach the paper to the jar. Every time you have change, put it in the jar. When the jar is full, empty it and donate it to charity. 30 POINTS

## ADOPT AN ANIMAL

You can "adopt" an animal that lives in the wild or in a local zoo or conservation area. This means sending money to support their habitats and the caregivers who look after them (in the wild) or for food and lodgings (if they are in a zoo). If you adopt an endangered animal in a zoo, then you might even be able to visit them!

> **YOUR 2-MINUTE MISSION:** **You could use your money to adopt an animal. Figure out how much you can save each week and then put it in your FOR FIGHTING EXTINCTION jar to use later to adopt your favorite animal. 20 POINTS**

## CAN'T DONATE MONEY? DONATE THINGS INSTEAD!

If you don't get an allowance or don't have money you can spare (it's OK—lots of people don't), then you could always donate your things or time to a charity that fights climate change. You could also look into volunteering locally.

**EVERYDAY SUPERHERO**

**Name:** Kurembera

**Job:** Mountain gorilla

**Superpower:** I have thick fur to survive in the mountains of Rwanda.

**How extinction affects you:** Disease (I can catch human diseases), war, and habitat loss

**Top tip:** Sponsor a mountain gorilla!

**Hates:** Traps set by humans that can kill or injure my friends

**Loves:** Living peacefully in the cloud forest

**KUREMBERA**

## RAISING FUNDS FOR ANIMALS

Lots of charities all over the world take care of many different types of animals through conservation work, by employing local rangers to keep them safe, or by doing research to find out how we can best look after them. These organizations need donations in order to keep doing this important work.

You can help by organizing fundraisers, doing sponsored events, or even holding a bake sale. It's a great way to make a difference right from home.

YOUR 2-MINUTE MISSION: Get together with your friends and have a superhero meeting to think up fundraising ideas to raise money for animal charities. 15 POINTS

## HOW ABOUT SOME OF THESE FUN IDEAS?

⚑ Set up a Superhero Car Wash.

⚑ Bake superhero cakes and sell them.

⚑ Organize a costume day at school and dress as your favorite endangered species.

⚑ Hold a garage sale.

⚑ Organize a 24-hour dance-off.

⚑ Hold a skateboard marathon.

⚑ Play Superhero Bingo.

GARAGE SALE

SUPER-HERO BINGO

Raising money isn't easy. But it can be done in all kinds of ways. You could ask people to sponsor you, set up a crowdfunding page, or do something as simple as pass around a donation box. It also doesn't have to be thousands that you raise. Every penny you raise will help animals in some way. And if it stops one, just one, from going extinct, then it's all worth it.

# FIGHT EXTINCTION WITH YOUR CLOTHES

How could what you wear possibly have anything to do with fighting extinction? Well, funnily enough, just like lots of other areas of life, what you wear has an effect on the planet.

The best news, though, is that you can do something about it.

Fashion uses up huge amounts of energy, takes up land to grow crops, takes up water to wash and make the clothes, or uses fossil fuels to make fabrics that do not degrade and that pollute the planet long after they have been worn.

## WHAT ARE YOU WEARING?

You might think of your clothes as just your clothes, right? Of course they are. But every item of clothing you or your parents or caregivers buy has an impact on the planet. Some are worse for the planet than others, so it's important to make clothing choices that help.

## FUR AND SKINS

It used to be fashionable to wear animal fur and animal skins. While you won't see many new clothes made from these today, the fashion industry still uses animals to make clothes.

People still wear shoes made out of snakeskin or carry handbags made from crocodiles. They might even have hats made from beavers. Many of these species are endangered.

## HOW "NATURAL" FIBERS CAUSE EXTINCTION

Rayon is a fabric that's made from wood pulp. In some countries, forest is cut down and native trees are used in this process. In other places, forest is cut down for farms, which is wrecking local biodiversity.

## HOW ARTIFICIAL FIBERS CAUSE EXTINCTION

Artificial fibers are made from fossil fuels. The fashion industry is extremely wasteful, uses up tons of energy, and produces huge amounts of carbon dioxide. This results in harmful levels of carbon dioxide. The long and short of it is that fashion—and particularly fast fashion, or cheap, mass-produced clothing—is bad for the planet and for nature.

# HOW DO YOU FIGHT EXTINCTION WITH YOUR CLOTHES?

Well, it's quite simple, really. All you have to do is stop buying new clothes, clothes made from artificial fibers like polyester and nylon, or clothes that use animal products, such as leather. There are lots of ways to do this and still be totally trendy. Here are some other fashion-friendly ideas to help you fight extinction—you super-stylish superhero!

**LEARN TO SEW:**
Making your own clothes isn't very easy. But learning how to sew will give you an amazing superpower: fixing things! It means your favorite clothes will live longer and have a happier life.

**SHOP SECONDHAND:**
Giving clothes a new life from a thrift store not only helps you save money but also helps reduce the demand for new clothes.

**YOUR 2-MINUTE MISSION:** Ask your parents, grandparents, or caregivers to teach you how to sew. Start with sewing on a button, then try something like mending a hole with a patch. **20 POINTS**

**YOUR 2-MINUTE MISSION:** Set yourself a ridiculously low budget—say, $10—and go clothes shopping at a thrift store. Get yourself a brand-new outfit for a party or even a costume party and save $$$, plus have fun! **20 POINTS**

**BUY ONCE AND WELL:**
Buy something from a brand committed to sustainable fashion practices, then wear it until it falls apart! But don't throw it out—repair it!

**SWAP YOUR STUFF:**
Your old clothes might be too small and unwanted by you, but they won't be to other people.

**REVAMP YOUR WARDROBE:**
Clothes that don't fit or that aren't exciting anymore can be revamped by sewing on patches, changing the buttons, or cutting off arms and legs!

**YOUR 2-MINUTE MISSION:** Save your money and then buy yourself something from a sustainable brand. It will help you to fight extinction by not buying lots of new stuff. **20 POINTS**

**YOUR 2-MINUTE MISSION:** Get your classmates to bring in all their unwanted clothes to school. Then swap! **20 POINTS**

# MISSION 13
# FIGHT EXTINCTION WITH YOUR VOICE

While some people say that actions speak louder than words, some superheroes are great at using their voice to protest and, as a result, make things happen. When it comes to extinctions, it's important to let the people who can make a difference know what needs to change.

If you are brave, people will listen.

It's not easy to stand up and use your voice. But sometimes that's what you have to do. Your teachers are very cool (did you know they are secret superheroes too?) and may allow you to speak at an all-school meeting or address your class, especially if it's about the welfare of the planet.

You can use your voice in lots of other ways too. Find out how in this chapter.

YOUR 2-MINUTE MISSION:
Write a song, rap, or poem. Many superheroes have used music and poetry to protest over the years.
20 POINTS

## START A CAMPAIGN

In 2018 Greta Thunberg decided to strike for climate change. Every Friday she went to the Swedish parliament and sat outside with a sign. Lots of people followed her, and in 2019 climate strikes took place all across the world. From one small action, Greta has influenced millions of people around the world to do the same and has been the voice of the young against a terrible threat.

You could do this too. But think about what you do carefully. Some adults won't like it if you miss school or disrupt "normal life" by protesting. So talk it through with your parents or caregivers and teachers, and make a protest that will enable you to use your voice with the support of your community. You may upset some people, but many more may agree with you.

### HOW TO BE A SUPERHERO ACTIVIST:

♠ Be prepared! Have your facts and data ready to share.

♠ Make signs and march around your playground.

♠ Set up a stall in your town center.

♠ Be clear about your aims.

♠ Be ready to explain why you are protesting.

♠ Don't damage property.

♠ Be ready to take action more than once. After all, it took Greta more than one Friday to get her movement started!

## LAUNCH A MOVEMENT

I started by doing a #2minutebeachclean every time I went to the beach. Now, some years later, my idea has turned into a foundation with lots of people supporting it and more than one thousand beach-cleaning stations along the coast.

> **YOUR 2-MINUTE MISSION: Start a club or a group to help nature. You could plant trees or recycle glass, plastics, and more! Celebrate doing good things for the planet. 30 POINTS**

## JOIN A MARCH

Talk to your family about going on a protest or march against extinction. You can find out times and details online. Tell them why you'd like to go and explain why you are worried about extinction, both here and abroad. Create a sign and make sure your voice gets heard!

> **YOUR 2-MINUTE MISSION: Make a sign. Write a message on it that explains what you are protesting for. Make it funny or emotional and very memorable. 20 POINTS**

## TIME TO TALK

Talking about extinction is the first step in getting anything done about it. But it is a BIG conversation. Try breaking things down so it's easier for people to understand.

- Explain what the problems are.
- Disarm them with some GREAT facts.
- Suggest what they can do to help.
- Start with something easy and simple.
- Offer an idea or project to work on together.
- Thank them for listening and thank them even more if they want to help!

YOUR 2-MINUTE MISSION: **Talk to your friends and family about how to help nature and animals at risk. 50 POINTS**

# FIGHT EXTINCTION AT SCHOOL

You spend a lot of time at school. In days it adds up to about half of your year. While you have to work hard studying, there is still plenty of time to fight extinction during your break times or in free periods. So why not?

You've already completed a lot of missions at home and in your backyard that will help fight extinction. Now it's time to take what you learned into school!

Your teachers, believe it or not, are superheroes too. Many of them care deeply about nature and the planet and will do their very best to make sure that the planet you inherit is happy and healthy. So please don't be afraid to talk to them. Show them this page and ask them to find some time to talk about extinction and nature.

## A MESSAGE FROM ME TO YOUR TEACHER

Dear Teacher,

Thanks for taking the time to read this. Your student has been reading this book because they care deeply about the environment and want to do their best to look after nature and the planet. They are, as you already know, on the road to becoming a superhero, and I'd love it if you could support them in this. Please listen to their concerns and work with them to make your school, and the planet, a place where nature can thrive.

Thank you,
Martin

## ⭐ EVERYDAY SUPERHERO ⭐

**Name:** Educator Extraordinaire

**Job:** Your teacher

**Superpower:** Making learning fun

**How you fight extinction:** I teach kids how to love nature and how to look after it.

**Top tip:** Listen to your teacher and thank them for teaching you.

**Hates:** When people don't listen to the concerns of my students

**Loves:** When kids fight extinction!

### TEACHER

**YOUR 2-MINUTE MISSION:** Hold an extinction assembly—it's a great time to talk to your schoolmates, even if it's a bit scary. But with the help of your friends, you could make it really fun and interesting for everyone. **20 POINTS**

## HELP ANIMALS AT SCHOOL

The more you can help your school to reduce the energy you use and the waste you create, the more you fight extinction and help animals and the planet!

## SAVE ENERGY

Your school uses energy to power the lights and the computers, and, just like at home, your school also produces waste, such as paper and plastic.

YOUR 2-MINUTE MISSION: **Talk to your principal about energy-efficient light bulbs, a recycling program, and composting in the cafeteria as ways your school might become greener. 10 POINTS**

## PAPER WASTE

Using less paper is a great way to fight extinction as it means less forest is cut down to make it. Forests that are specially grown to make paper are usually lacking in biodiversity—because they contain only one type of tree—and take up land that should be natural forest where nature can thrive.

YOUR 2-MINUTE MISSION: **Save paper—and trees. Try to print out fewer things and print double-sided to save paper. Write on both sides of a piece of paper and recycle when you're done! 10 POINTS**

## PLASTIC WASTE

Plastic is dangerous for wildlife if it gets into the environment. If you use less of it, you'll be helping to fight extinction, because every piece of plastic has an adverse effect on nature.

YOUR 2-MINUTE MISSION: **Talk to your teacher and classmates and encourage them to use less plastic at school. 10 POINTS**

## FOOD WASTE

You can help fight extinction even on your lunch break. Reducing food waste will help save the energy needed to dispose of it at a recycling facility, where it may produce methane, a greenhouse gas, as it breaks down. You can also reduce the use of those pesky single-use plastics that you might find in your lunch box, such as plastic straws and zip-top bags.

YOUR 2-MINUTE MISSION: **Save on food waste by eating all of your lunch—yum! If you can't eat it all, ask for smaller portions. 10 POINTS**

YOUR 2-MINUTE MISSION: **Reduce the plastic in your lunch by using reusable containers. 10 POINTS**

# JOIN YOUR SCHOOL'S STUDENT COUNCIL

I'm sorry to say, but it's the grown-ups who are causing extinctions. I don't mean it's your parents or teachers. I mean the people in charge of the planet, such as politicians and corporations, who don't think of nature and the environment first.

How can you change this? You can start by joining your student council. As a member of student government, you will get to have a say in how your school is run. That means you'll be able to make sure that the subject of extinction is talked about and acted upon. After that, aim even higher. We could use people in government who take action on extinction. That could be you! Why? Because you are a superhero.

**YOUR 2-MINUTE MISSION:** Join your student council to help change the rules so you can fight extinction and speak up for nature. If your school doesn't have a student council, start one. You have the right to have a say! 50 POINTS

# LET NATURE INTO YOUR SCHOOL

Schools are great places for nature to thrive, if you let it. There are so many things you could do to help your school grounds become a wildlife haven, a refuge for birds, and a dinner table for insects. Even if you live in a city, there are things you can do to let nature into your school!

**YOUR 2-MINUTE MISSION: Talk to your teacher and classmates about planning a wildlife area for plants, insects, and animals to find a home. 20 POINTS**

**Try the ideas below! Some of them might not be right for your school. However, discussing each item will help bring it to the attention of your class and will start to make a difference.**

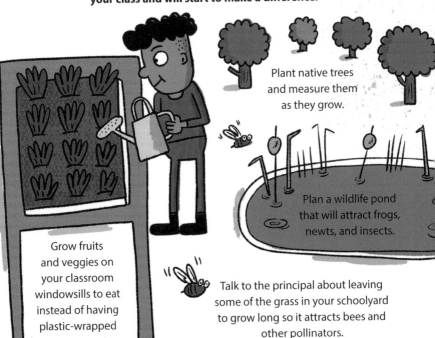

Plant native trees and measure them as they grow.

Plan a wildlife pond that will attract frogs, newts, and insects.

Grow fruits and veggies on your classroom windowsills to eat instead of having plastic-wrapped lettuce or tomatoes.

Talk to the principal about leaving some of the grass in your schoolyard to grow long so it attracts bees and other pollinators.

# FIGHT EXTINCTION WHEN YOU TRAVEL

The average superhero gets around quite a bit. You travel to school and to stores, and sometimes you even get to go on vacation (because superheroes need a break, right?). How you do this, and what you do when you get there, can make a real difference to the natural world.

## GOING TO SCHOOL

While you might not think traveling by car has much to do with extinctions, it's still relevant. Traveling by car creates greenhouse gases and pollution that affect the whole planet. And that is one factor that's affecting nature all over the world. So the less you travel by car, the better.

YOUR 2-MINUTE MISSION: If it's possible to walk to school, try it for one day a week. Could you meet up with friends to walk together and create a "walking bus"? Each day you walk instead of riding in the car helps save the planet (and makes you healthier too!). 20 POINTS

YOUR 2-MINUTE MISSION: Cycling is another really efficient way of traveling that doesn't harm the planet. See if your school or park district offers bike safety lessons. If not, talk to someone about getting a course started! 20 POINTS

## PLANE:

Per passenger, planes give off the most carbon per mile. So don't go to school in your private jet. Not even if you have one!

## TRAIN:

Trains use less fuel per passenger than cars. Let the train take the strain!

## BUS:

Better than traveling by car. Less pollution, traffic, and carbon is better for the planet!

## CAR:

Cars produce emissions and pollution and use fossil fuels. Not so great for the planet and nature.

## FEET OR WHEELCHAIR:

Fantastic! Just don't tread on any creepy-crawlies!

## BICYCLE:

Amazing. You power the bike with your own energy!

## GOING ON VACATION

Traveling, whether by car, train, or plane, creates greenhouse gases and contributes to climate change. As we know, this is having an adverse effect on animals everywhere, endangering them and contributing to extinctions. So, to fight extinction, we must also fight climate change.

Going on vacation can create a lot of greenhouse gases, especially if you're traveling very far. But your superhero fight doesn't stop just because you are on vacation. You can still do lots to help animals and nature even when you're away from home. And remember, the less you travel by car, the better.

### ⭐ EVERYDAY SUPERHERO ⭐

**Name:** Olly

**Job:** Orca

**Superpower:** I am called a killer whale, but I'm not a whale! I'm a huge dolphin.

**How extinction affects you:** I am a victim of chemicals in seawater.

**Top tip:** Try to use fewer chemicals in your bathroom and garden.

**Hates:** Chemicals in the water

**Loves:** Swimming around, catching seals, eating well

OLLY

# THE AMAZING EXTINCTIONCATION

Staycations are vacations you take at home. They help fight extinction because you don't create as many greenhouse gases when you don't use transportation. Pretend you are in a hotel and have a big breakfast before going out to explore nature near you.

> YOUR 2-MINUTE MISSION: **Talk to your parents or caregivers about your next vacation and doing something that's planet positive. 40 POINTS**

Visit animal rescues and sanctuaries that save animals.

Do a #2minutebeachclean or #2minutelitterpick.

Make it a plastic-free vacation:

Bring your water bottle, metal straw, and reusable bags!

Try eco-friendly activities. (Sorry, no Jet Skis!)

# FIGHT EXTINCTION WITH YOUR PEN

Your last task is about being creative with words and pictures to help the animals. The pen is mightier than the sword, and you have the power to tell the people in charge or the people who make the rules what needs to change. Use your pens and pencils to fight extinction.

> **YOUR 2-MINUTE MISSION:** Draw a poster to put up in school about animals or plants that are in danger near you. Make the poster exciting and visual so that your teachers and classmates see it and will be compelled to act. **50 POINTS**

Dear [insert name of president, congressperson, or city councilor here],

My name is [INSERT YOUR NAME HERE]. I am [YOUR AGE HERE]. I am writing to you because I am worried about extinction, biodiversity loss, and the destruction of natural habitats.

I have taken lots of actions in the fight against extinction. [LIST THEM HERE] I have built a bee hotel so that our local bee population can find a home. I have also persuaded my parents to stop mowing our lawn as often so that insects can find food. I have helped to build a pond for wildlife at my school. I have also spoken to my friends and family about extinction.

I have done all I can. But I can't make important decisions about how our society treats nature or pass laws that halt the illegal wildlife trade or that encourage rewilding. I can't ban plastic packaging and single-use plastics. I can't control the use of pesticides and bee-killing chemicals. I can't designate marine protection zones or stop destructive road- or rail-building projects. I can't talk to foreign leaders and agree on the protection of animals and nature.

But you can. While you might not feel the full effects of climate change and extinctions in your lifetime, I will. That's why I'd like you to pledge to do more to protect nature and the environment in order to avoid this global crisis.

Yours, [SIGN HeRE]

# MISSION COMPLETED

Now that you have completed your missions, it's time to look back at what you have achieved and what effect it may have had. First, though, I'd like to thank you for all the work you have done, on behalf of the natural world. It means your future could be in a world that is full of nature, wonder, and biodiversity, on a healthy planet where humans and wildlife live happily side by side. How wonderful!

Imagine yourself in harmony with the planet, riding your bike, eating great food, loving life, and having fun. The skies are full of birds, the meadows are full of flowers and buzzing with bees and other insects, and the rivers are clear and cool and full of fish.

You helped to do that!

You've talked to friends and family about the crisis in nature to raise awareness.

You've saved up to sponsor an animal at your local zoo or donated a bit of your money to conservation charities. You might even have done a sponsored event for them too. Go, you!

You've grown a meadow in your garden for bees and insects by persuading your parents to mow less often.

You've planted a tree that will become a home for thousands of tiny creatures, birds, and insects.

You've given bees the food and homes they deserve so they can pollinate our crops.

You've found out what's in your food and what a difference it makes to the planet to avoid some ingredients. Hopefully you've said goodbye to palm oil FOREVER!

You've written a song and had a hit record (well, nearly) and you've written to the president. That's a BIG DEAL.

It all adds up to make a difference, and when you combine it with all the work the other superheroes have done, it's HUGE. So let's keep spreading the word. Let's not stop until we've made a difference and nature is restored.

You will be able to find your superhero rating on the following pages, but for now, let's cheer to you, THE SUPERHERO, for helping to save nature and carry the message far and wide.

You are my hero.

**Thank you,**

**Martin**

# YOUR
# SUPERHERO
# RATING . . .

# SUPERHERO POINTS

Now that you've finished your training, it's time to discover what kind of superhero you are. Add up the points you've earned by completing your missions.

## MISSION 1: GET TO KNOW EXTINCTION

Use your superhero ability of discovery to go on a fossil hunt! **10 POINTS**

Go to the park, the country, or even just your backyard. Sit quietly for a couple of minutes and see if you can spot a dinosaur. (CLUE: Birds are distant relatives of dinosaurs.) **5 POINTS**

**TOTAL MISSION POINTS: 15**

## MISSION 3: THE PLANET IN THE BALANCE

Make a terrarium. It is a self-sustaining ecosystem. It's pretty easy to make one, although you might need some help from an adult. **15 POINTS**

Draw your own food chain. It could be real or imagined, and it will help you understand the link between one animal and the next. What will eat what? Are they dinosaurs? Elephants? Sharks? Dolphins? GO WILD! **5 POINTS**

**TOTAL MISSION POINTS: 20**

## MISSION 4: FIGHT EXTINCTION FROM THE GROUND UP

Go outside and see if you can find any creepy-crawlies. Don't get too close or touch them. Replace any stones carefully and try not to harm any of your creepy-crawly friends. **10 POINTS**

Get to know your creepy-crawlies better. Books can help you identify insects. Apps are great at helping you find out what they do and how they act. (Beware: some may have in-app purchases.) **5 POINTS**

Weed killer is terrible for insects and invertebrates. Ask your caregivers, school, and town to stop using it, if they do. You can write letters and emails or even start a protest. **10 POINTS**

Name your pet spider. Spiders are great. So next time you find one, don't harm it. Give it a name, let it do its thing, and be its friend. **10 POINTS**

Inspire your friends to take care of insects too. Could you dress up like an insect? Or maybe you could write a story about your pet spider? **10 POINTS**

**TOTAL MISSION POINTS: 45**

## MISSION 5: FIGHT EXTINCTION IN THE GARDEN

Can you see plants growing in the cracks in the sidewalk, in gaps between bricks, and in spaces that are unloved or forgotten? Isn't it amazing how nature always seems to find a way to grow—no matter how hard we make it! **5 POINTS**

Take this book outside and see if you can spot any invasive species. If it's Japanese knotweed, you'll need to tell an adult. It is on the National Park Service's Targeted Plant Species Watchlist, and eradicating it requires special techniques. **10 POINTS**

Download a plant identification app. Then go out into the garden or park and try to identify a few plants. Are they considered weeds? Are they friend or foe? You decide, based on how you think they help the natural world. **10 POINTS**

In the autumn, plant a bee-friendly flowerpot with bulbs of crocus, snowdrop, grape hyacinth, and scented daffodil. The bulbs will produce flowers in the spring when the bees need them most. **30 POINTS**

Make a bee hotel. **50 POINTS**

Let dandelions grow in your garden. Dandelions are among the first flowers to bloom in spring.

That means bees can feast on nectar soon after a long winter or hibernation. **10 POINTS**

Talk to the mower in your family about mowing every three weeks instead of every week. **10 POINTS**

Want to earn some money and help save the planet? Offer to mow the lawn! If you raise the cutting blades to their maximum height (get an adult to help with this), it will help insects and birds. **20 POINTS**

Make a flyer to put in the mailboxes on your street asking people to cut down their mowing from once a week to once every three weeks. Make it colorful and don't forget to include facts from this book.
**10 POINTS**

**TOTAL MISSION POINTS: 155**

## MISSION 6: FIGHT EXTINCTION AT THE BIRDFEEDER

Make a seed cake for the birds to eat! It's really easy (but you might need to get a little help from one of your pet adults). **30 POINTS**

Make a bird café. It can be as simple as hanging seed cakes off a hook on your balcony. But if you have help and a few bits of wood, it's easy.
**50 POINTS**

Take a book out of the library or download an app and learn to identify the birds that visit your bird café. **10 POINTS**

**TOTAL MISSION POINTS: 90**

## MISSION 7: FIGHT EXTINCTION WITH WATER

Harvesting rainwater is really easy to do. Put out a bucket on your windowsill, on the balcony, or in your backyard, and see how much water you collect when it rains. Save it and use it to water your plants, either indoors or outdoors, when they need it. **10 POINTS**

Speak to your parents or caregivers about setting up a water barrel. If you grow plants, it will be useful for watering them. **10 POINTS**

Make a simple pond by using an old bowl. **10 POINTS**

**TOTAL MISSION POINTS: 30**

## MISSION 8: FIGHT EXTINCTION IN THE SUPERMARKET

Find a food that your family eats regularly. Check out the ingredients. If it has GMOs or palm oil in it, find an alternative, if you can. Do a price comparison. Is it cheaper or more expensive? **10 POINTS**

Add organic material, such as compost, to your garden. Worms are

the heroes of the mud. They recycle dead matter—like leaves and dead flowers—and turn it into healthy, nutrient-rich soil that's great for growing. **20 POINTS**

While you might not be able to change what food your family buys, you can look at the labels in your house. Check them out and see where your food comes from. Take a look at some of the ingredients you're consuming. **10 POINTS**

Check the labels of foods you suspect may have soy. If the soy is from Brazil, try to avoid it or find another option. **10 POINTS**

Look at the labels on your groceries. See if you can spot the palm oil. **10 POINTS**

**TOTAL MISSION POINTS: 60**

## MISSION 9: FIGHT EXTINCTION IN THE KITCHEN

Berries are grown all over the world. There are many varieties that are native to North America. See if you can find them in your local stores. **10 POINTS**

Look at your favorite fish dish and then go and look it up at https://www.seafoodwatch.org /recommendations to see how your fish fared. Did it do OK? Great! Not

so good? Maybe it's time to change brands or try something different.
**20 POINTS**

Go vegan for a day. I bet you'll find that you love being a plant-based superhero. If you like it, why not go vegan one day each week?
**50 POINTS**

Make oat milk and try it on your cereal. It's the very best milk for the planet. **40 POINTS**

**TOTAL MISSION POINTS: 120**

## MISSION 10: FIGHT EXTINCTION IN THE BATHROOM

Check out your bathroom products and discover which ones are planet-friendly and which ones are not. Look for palm oil, plastic, preservatives, and unsustainable ingredients. See if you can spot the RSPO logo on any product. **10 POINTS**

Visit a zero-waste store. They have lots of products that are plastic-free and good for the planet. Look for soap that doesn't contain palm oil and shampoo bars that you can rub on your head! **20 POINTS**

Done your missions? Good. Now it's time to have some superhero fun. Relax with an eco-friendly, homemade, luxury bath bomb.
**50 POINTS**

**TOTAL MISSION POINTS: 80**

## MISSION 11: FIGHT EXTINCTION WITH YOUR MONEY

Find an empty glass jar and a piece of recycled or reused paper. Write FOR FIGHTING EXTINCTION on the paper and then use string or biodegradable tape to attach the paper to the jar. Every time you have change, put it in the jar. When the jar is full, empty it and donate it to charity. **30 POINTS**

You could use your money to adopt an animal. Figure out how much you can save each week and then put it in your FOR FIGHTING EXTINCTION jar to use later to adopt your favorite animal.
**20 POINTS**

Get together with your friends and have a superhero meeting to think up fundraising ideas to raise money for animal charities.
**15 POINTS**

**TOTAL MISSION POINTS: 65**

## MISSION 12: FIGHT EXTINCTION WITH YOUR CLOTHES

Ask your parents, grandparents, or caregivers to teach you how to sew. Start with sewing on a button, then try something like mending a hole with a patch. **20 POINTS**

Set yourself a ridiculously low budget—say, $10—and go clothes

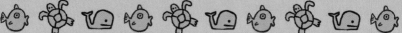

shopping at a thrift store. Get yourself a brand-new outfit for a party or even a costume party and save $$$, plus have fun! **20 POINTS**

Save your money and then buy yourself something from a sustainable brand. It will help you to fight extinction by not buying lots of new stuff. **20 POINTS**

Get your classmates to bring in all their unwanted clothes to school. Then swap! **20 POINTS**

**TOTAL MISSION POINTS: 80**

## MISSION 13: FIGHT EXTINCTION WITH YOUR VOICE

Write a song, rap, or poem. Many superheroes have used music and poetry to protest over the years. **20 POINTS**

Start a club or a group to help nature. You could plant trees or recycle glass, plastics, and more! Celebrate doing good things for the planet. **30 POINTS**

Make a sign. Write a message on it that explains what you are protesting for. Make it funny or emotional and very memorable. **20 POINTS**

Talk to your friends and family about how to help nature and animals at risk. **50 POINTS**

**TOTAL MISSION POINTS: 120**

## MISSION 14: FIGHT EXTINCTION AT SCHOOL

Hold an extinction assembly— it's a great time to talk to your schoolmates, even if it's a bit scary. But with the help of your friends, you could make it really fun and interesting for everyone. **20 POINTS**

Talk to your principal about energy-efficient light bulbs, a recycling program, and composting in the cafeteria as ways your school might become greener. **10 POINTS**

Save paper—and trees. Try to print out fewer things and print double-sided to save paper. Write on both sides of a piece of paper and recycle when you're done! **10 POINTS**

Talk to your teacher and classmates and encourage them to use less plastic at school. **10 POINTS**

Save on food waste by eating all of your lunch—yum! If you can't eat it all, ask for smaller portions. **10 POINTS**

Make your lunches plastic-free by using reusable containers. **10 POINTS**

Join your student council to help change the rules so you can fight extinction and speak up for nature. If your school doesn't have a student council, start one. You have the right to have a say! **50 POINTS**

Talk to your teacher and classmates about planning a wildlife area for plants, insects, and animals to find a home. **20 POINTS**

**TOTAL MISSION POINTS: 140**

## MISSION 15: FIGHT EXTINCTION WHEN YOU TRAVEL

If it's possible to walk to school, try it for one day a week. Could you meet up with friends to walk together and create a "walking bus"? Each day you walk instead of riding in the car helps save the planet (and makes you healthier too!).
**20 POINTS**

Cycling is another really efficient way of traveling that doesn't harm the planet. See if your school or park district offers bike safety lessons. If not, talk to someone about getting a course started! **20 POINTS**

Talk to your parents or caregivers about your next vacation and doing something that's planet positive.
**40 POINTS**

**TOTAL MISSION POINTS: 80**

## BONUS MISSION: FIGHT EXTINCTION WITH YOUR PEN

Draw a poster to put up in school about animals or plants that are in danger near you. Make the poster exciting and visual so that your teachers see it and will be compelled to act. **50 POINTS**

Write a letter to someone important who can act on a global scale. You can use this template to write to the president of the United States, but you could also write to your state or local government. **100 POINTS**

**TOTAL MISSION POINTS: 150**

# WHAT KIND OF SUPERHERO ARE YOU?

Now that you have completed the missions, take a look at what kind of superhero you are. How did you do? Well, actually, can I let you in on a secret? It doesn't really matter. The most important thing is that you do something, anything, to fight extinction.

You are amazing!

## 0–499 POINTS

Fantastic! You have done so well to come this far, you superhero in the making. I applaud your commitment and urge you to keep going! With just a few more tasks under your belt, you'll be well on the road to Gold Star Superhero status. Mind you, the work you have done to date will add up to make a difference, and that's what matters. Go, you. Go, nature. We are winning!

**MISSION COMPLETE: You're a 3 ★ Superhero!**

## 500–999 POINTS

Hey there. You are doing an awesome job. Stardust awaits you. By doing a few simple things to help nature, you have shown true commitment. I am so glad to have you on our team. With your help, the natural world is getting a boost.

**MISSION COMPLETE: You're a real 4 ★ Superhero!**

You rock. Thanks to your work—and your work talking to others—you are making a difference. You are a true, top-notch superhero, and I am proud to know you. You aren't just on the team—you are leading from the front and setting the very best example. Fabulous work.

**MISSION COMPLETE: You get the 5 ★ Superhero Award!**

IMAGINE YOUR PHOTO HERE

EVERYDAY SUPERHERO

What's your name?

What's your job?

What's your superpower?

How do you fight extinction?

What's your top tip?

What do you hate?

What do you love?

YOU

# FIND OUT MORE ABOUT THE FIGHT AGAINST EXTINCTION

**Want to find out how to get involved? Great! Take a look at these:**

**The World Wildlife Fund:** A charity with lots of information and online resources for superheroes
**www.worldwildlife.org**

**Defenders of Wildlife:** A US nonprofit that works to protect wildlife and restore native habitats
**https://defenders.org**

**International Union for Conservation of Nature:** An international organization that monitors species to help protect nature
**www.iucn.org**

**Extinction Rebellion:** Look for family events and local family groups.
**https://www.extinctionrebellion.us**

**The National Wildlife Federation:** A US organization that provides guidance on contacting state and local officials so you can help spread the word about extinction
**www.nwf.org/Our-Work/Wildlife-Conservation /Endangered-Species**